# SCALE

## How to Grow Your Business by Working Less

BY FRANK BRIA

Printed in the United States of America


First Printing, 2015


ISBN 978-0-9857254-5-7


Cambio Publishing
3317 S Higley Rd
Suite 114-335
Gilbert, AZ 85297
www.frankbria.com

# Introduction

What is holding you back?

Many a service professional has reported the frustrating experiencing of not being able to disconnect from their business. Many entrepreneurs are miserable because the thing they created has turned into the very job they tried to escape. Many a business owner has discovered that their business has grown so large and become so busy that they are now trapped by their own success.

Has this happened to you?

A scalable business makes it possible to create passive income and grow the business by *actually working less*. But as you do less work, you do so more thoughtfully, more connected to the value you really offer your business. It takes effort on your part to evaluate each of the **Four Keys to Scale** discussed in this book.

You will need to be willing to re-think your business. You will need to change what you're doing. There are no shortcuts to scale.

But there is a roadmap.

Imagine what your life would be like if your business could earn money without you. What would that change in your life?

Would you go on more vacations? Would you spend more time with loved ones? Would you pursue personal hobbies that are just a dream right now? Would you leave your cellphone at home?

*Scale* is a ticket to freedom masquerading as a business book.

Are you ready to get your ticket?

# Book Upgrades

Throughout the book, there are a number of places where online resources are available.

As a thank you for purchasing the book, I'm offering you **free video training** on how to grow your business to 7-figures! This is training I charge thousands of dollars for, but I want to give it to you as a "kickstart" to your effort to scale.

You can get those resources as an owner of the book by registering your book at:

http://scalebookoffer.com

There you will find checklists for the chapters, video training, and group programs to support you in your efforts to scale your business.

You can even join our Facebook group, Scale. It's free and it's a great place for people like you to connect with other entrepreneurs facing similar issues of Scale.

# Dedication

It's been my experience that you don't write a book alone.

Besides the people who have contributed to the content including Sarah Thompson and Mel West, dozens of people have reacted to versions of the draft and given me great feedback along the way.

This book is a direct result of my experience in changing my business model from a consultant to a true business owner. That change hasn't been easy. And not just on me, but on my family as well.

Through it all have been my three daughters and my wife. With every question they got from on-lookers of the sort, "what exactly is he doing now," they answered with pride. As best they could.

Much of this book is about transformation and finding out what you're meant to do in this world. It's a messy but necessary process. And for those looking on from the wings, sometimes it's a bit scary. Thank you to my family and friends for hanging in with me during it all.

My wife deserves the credit for the person – and businessperson – I've become. Without her support and love, none of this would be possible. Nor would any of it matter.

I love you.

# Table of Contents

**SECTION 1. THE CASE FOR SCALE** ........................................... 1

CHAPTER 1. WHY SCALE AT ALL? ................................................ 2
*The "Growth Ceiling"* ................................................................ 2
*Why Scale?* ............................................................................... 4
*The Benefits of a Scalable Business* ........................................... 5
*Four Keys to Scale* .................................................................... 6
*Principles of Scale Can Help Struggling Businesses* ..................... 8
*Fire You!* ................................................................................ 10
CHAPTER 2. WHAT IS SCALE? ................................................... 13
*To Scale is Human* ................................................................. 13
*Why Can't You Just Grow As Is?* ............................................. 14
*The Goal: Decreasing Marginal Costs* ...................................... 17

**SECTION 2. THE CONCEPT** ..................................................... 21

CHAPTER 3. THE OFFER ........................................................... 22
*Target Market* ........................................................................ 22
*One Big Problem* ..................................................................... 24
*One Big Result* ........................................................................ 28
CHAPTER 4. THE CUSTOMER .................................................... 33
*Identifying Your Customer Profile* .......................................... 33
*Customer Demographics* .......................................................... 34
*Customer Psychographics* ........................................................ 36
*How Many Profiles Are Too Many? (Or Too Few?)* .................. 39
*B2C and B2B Examples* ........................................................... 40
CHAPTER 5. AUDIENCE SEGMENTS .......................................... 45
*What is a "Need Segment?"* ...................................................... 45
CHAPTER 6. THE MESSAGING ................................................... 56
*Audience Connections* ............................................................. 56
*Key Prospect Messages* ............................................................ 56

*Key Customer Messages* ........................................................ *60*
*Audience Channels* ............................................................... *63*

## SECTION 3. THE BUSINESS MODEL .......................... **73**

### CHAPTER 7. MONETIZATION .................................... **74**
*The Goal: New Stable and Recurring Revenue* ....................... *74*
*Creating New Revenue* ......................................................... *76*
*Creating Diverse Revenue* ..................................................... *77*
*Creating Recurring Revenue* ................................................. *79*
*Creating Stable Revenue* ....................................................... *81*

### CHAPTER 8. CREATING AND REFINING YOUR PRODUCT ..... **85**
*Get Ready for Imperfection* ................................................... *85*
*Get Minimal* ....................................................................... *87*
*Get Viable* ........................................................................... *90*
*Launch Now. No, Really; Now.* .............................................. *92*

### CHAPTER 9. APPROPRIATE PRICING ......................... **97**
*Scalable Pricing Models* ....................................................... *97*
*Pricing for Profitability* ........................................................ *99*
*Pricing for Availability* ....................................................... *101*
*Pricing for Market Need* ..................................................... *102*

### CHAPTER 10. CASH FLOW PLANNING ...................... **106**
*Cash Flow Formula* ............................................................ *106*
*Borrowing and Investment* ................................................. *107*
*Bootstrapping* .................................................................... *110*
*Spending and Budgeting* ..................................................... *113*

## SECTION 4. THE MARKET ...................................... **117**

### CHAPTER 11. BUILDING LOYALTY ........................... **118**
*What is the Loyalty Ladder?* ................................................ *118*
*Building Your Loyalty Ladder* ............................................. *121*

### CHAPTER 12. MARKETING & ADVERTISING CAMPAIGNS ..... **125**
*The Difference between Marketing & Advertising* ................... *125*
*The Four Calls-to-Action* .................................................... *125*
*When to Use Each* .............................................................. *130*
*Creating Advertising & Marketing Copy* .............................. *131*
*Internet as a Strategy* ......................................................... *132*
*Content Marketing as a Strategy* ......................................... *134*

*Sales as a Strategy* ............................................................... *137*

CHAPTER 13. MANAGING METRICS ...................................142

*Importance of Metrics* ........................................................... *142*

*Response Rates and Migration Rates* ..................................... *145*

*Customer Lifetime Value (CLV)* ............................................ *148*

*Expected Revenue Levels (ERL)* ............................................ *148*

CHAPTER 14. THE PLATFORM ............................................156

*What is a Marketing Platform?* .............................................. *156*

*Add Channels* ...................................................................... *158*

*Enlarge Your Tribe* .............................................................. *164*

*Broaden Niche* ..................................................................... *165*


SECTION 5. THE PROCESSES ....................................169

CHAPTER 15. MARKETING AUTOMATION .........................170

*Lead Generation* .................................................................. *170*

*Prospect Communication* ...................................................... *172*

*Customer Service* ................................................................. *174*

*Up-Selling, Cross-Selling, and Referrals* ............................... *176*

CHAPTER 16. SALES EXECUTION ......................................182

*The Role of Sales in Marketing* ............................................. *182*

*Where Sales Belongs in the Loyalty Ladder* ........................... *184*

*Learning to Close to the Next Step* ........................................ *186*

*Moving from Sales Back to "Care and Feeding"* ..................... *187*

CHAPTER 17. OPERATIONS ...............................................191

*Defining How You Operate* ................................................... *191*

*Coordinating with a Team* ................................................... *195*

*Improving the Process* .......................................................... *198*

CHAPTER 18. THE PEOPLE ...............................................205

*Hiring* ................................................................................. *205*

*Training* .............................................................................. *207*

*Leadership* ........................................................................... *209*

*Problem Resolution* .............................................................. *212*

*Dismissal* ............................................................................ *215*


SECTION 6. THE NEW ROAD .....................................219

CHAPTER 19. FEEDBACK AND CHANGE ............................220

*Continuous Improvement* ..................................................... *220*

*Feedback from the Market* ..................................................................*223*

*Organizational Change Model* ..........................................................*226*

CHAPTER 20. ACHIEVING SCALE ..................................... **231**

*The Next Growth Ceiling* ..................................................................*231*

*Your Next 90 Days* ...........................................................................*233*

*Step 1. Identify your blind spot.* ........................................................*233*

*Step 2. Fill the Hole* ........................................................................*234*

*Step 3. Build the Plan* ......................................................................*236*

*Step 4. Make It Happen!* ...................................................................*236*

ABOUT THE AUTHOR ..................................................... **238**

# Section 1. The Case for Scale

# Chapter 1. Why Scale at All?

## The "Growth Ceiling"

I remember the day it hit me. I had been in India the day before. Though groggy and exhausted from my flight, I had had an entire day of meetings – from 9:00 a.m. through 10:00 p.m. – and after the meetings ended, I still needed to interview people to fill open consulting positions. But the next morning, I hopped on a plane to Ukraine.

I was in Kiev when I got a call from my wife. She was in the hospital, having driven herself there during the middle of the night. She hadn't realized quite how ill she was, but in fact she needed surgery. Meanwhile, I was halfway around the world, and my children, who fortunately weren't very young, were alone. But they had to get themselves fed, and off to school; their mother was in the hospital and their father was far from home. I felt helpless, and like a terrible husband and father. It took me three days to get home, three days during which I thought about the price of success.

Although I had created the successful business I had aspired to create, I was trapped. I couldn't make personal time for anything that was important to me if I expected to deliver the products and services I had promised to my clients. My physical presence was required, and there was no substitute. No one could fill in for me; no one could take my place. Of course, this gave me job security, but it came at the cost of not being able to take a vacation or nothing would get done. I was living the life of a successful businessman, but it was not the life that I had intended.

My physical presence was required at home, too. While I was on the road, I missed seeing my children grow up, let alone participating in their development. The concept of scale had become personal for me.

Why should you listen to me? I have had fifteen years of experience helping financial services, technology, and retail companies start up new businesses, get their products to market, and grow organizations. With *Scale*, I am sharing with you the "secrets" I have shared with Fortune 500 and tech startup companies so you can apply them to your own company.

What had happened to me occurs to many entrepreneurs and business owners when they discover that their business has grown so large and become so busy that they have become trapped by their own success. Has this happened to you?

There are two problems associated with this. First, it creates a lifestyle that is simply not fun. It's not what most entrepreneurs aspire to when they decide to become their own bosses. When people create businesses, they generally use words like "freedom" and "autonomy," but once you create a business that requires direct involvement, those concepts are the last things you actually get to experience.

The second problem is a fact of human nature. Most people are not happy unless they're making progress. Business owners want to see growth, but by creating a business that relies on your presence, you may have guaranteed your job security but you have also limited your business' growth; you have hit the Growth Ceiling. The business cannot grow beyond your own ability to service your clients.

*In the beginning, a business may grow very quickly, with hockey-stick-shaped projections and amazing sales figures, month after month. At some point, however, this growth necessarily slows down and flattens out.*

The Growth Ceiling occurs in every business and in every industry. In fact, as a business grows, it hits multiple Growth Ceilings because they occur at multiple stages. In order to grow a business with a sustainable growth trajectory, and achieve the lifestyle to which most entrepreneurs and small business owners aspire, you have to scale.

This requires work because you must fight two laws of nature – entropy and metamorphosis – that cause businesses to get stuck under these Growth Ceilings.

The first is the law of entropy: moving toward chaos. Unless you make some fundamental changes in your business, it will become more and more expensive to achieve continued growth. This concept confuses most because they believe that "the bigger you are, the bigger you can become," as if this happens by 'magic.' Nothing in the natural world works that way; systems have a tendency to move toward chaos, not order. Without explicit effort, your business will grow more chaotic and it will become harder and harder to achieve growth.

The second is the law of metamorphosis: a change in physical form or structure. The business you built when you started is not the business you can grow. It's a simple fact that the dynamics that enabled you to start a company from scratch are not the dynamics that will propel it into the next level of growth. In much the same way that a caterpillar must go through the chrysalis stage before becoming a butterfly, your business must undergo a metamorphosis of scale in order to evolve into something beautiful and with greater skills and potential.

## Why Scale?

How would you like to run a business that had a passive income stream? If you struggle to meet payroll month after month or seasonally, or have to hold off investing in new technology or systems because the business isn't generating enough cash at the moment, the idea of passive income probably sounds pretty good. Even if your business is running profitably, passive income should be appealing because it doesn't cannibalize your current sales efforts.

That is the great advantage of scale. By evaluating and manipulating the Four Keys to Scale that are described below, you should be able to *transform your business into one that generates a passive income stream while reducing your cost of doing business.*

## The Benefits of a Scalable Business

Early in my consulting career, I had a client who was eager to grow her business. I asked her, "What's the vision of the life you want to create through your business?" She answered, "I want to be able to sit in my hot tub, with my laptop nearby, and watch the money roll into my bank account."

At first, I laughed at the idea, but in fact that is truly the promise of a scalable business. Although every business requires continual involvement and effort, it shouldn't require as much work as the business requires today. On the other hand, as a business grows, it tends to require more effort, so how can scale address that problem?

A scalable business makes it possible to create passive income *and* grow the business by doing less – but doing so more thoughtfully. It takes effort on your part to truly evaluate each of the Four Keys of Scale and make the appropriate changes in order to yield those benefits. The promise of scale is being able to earn more while doing less.

This seems like a contradictory concept and requires us to rethink how we operate.

Imagine what your life would be like if you could earn money without having to exercise the same amount of effort that you expend today.

What if, like I was, you are in a business that is entirely dependent on you and your presence to generate income? If you don't work, you don't earn. Imagine transforming that business into one in which the earning takes place even *without* your direct involvement; you can, in fact, sit in the hot tub and watch the money roll into your bank account.

Even a scaled business will hit a growth ceiling later in its future that will require re-evaluating the Four Keys to Scale. Perhaps it's a business in which you spend your time managing the processes that deliver those services instead of delivering the actual services. You may still find that you've "maxed out" your capacity to manage the processes. That is when you need to go through the exercise of creating scale, again, by bringing in processes, people and policies that allow you to be less involved in the day-to-day operations of delivering your product or service.

If you find yourself in that situation, imagine having trusted advisers who manage operations day-to–day, allowing you to focus on a strategic direction of your business. As you bring in different people, different products, different processes, and different cash-flow models, you will grow your business in ways you didn't think possible. This is the potential in creating scale. This is why it's important to understand why it's necessary to have the Four Keys to Scale in place.

## Four Keys to Scale

In my work with companies around the world, I have found that there are Four Keys to successfully scaling a business. Generally speaking, the idea is to position your product, price and monetize it in a way to gain customers, develop access to markets, and enable the continued growth of your company through solid processes.

The first Key involves identifying the **Concept** behind the business. This refers to knowing what product or service the company delivers, to which market, and the benefit it delivers. This needs to be defined in a way that allows the business to grow.

It may seem obvious, but a business needs to have a Concept that is open to scaling. Certain business concepts cannot scale, while other businesses that have been successful up to a certain level of revenues will have to change their Concept in order to continue to grow.

We'll discuss in future sections what goes into creating a Concept that can Scale, and understanding when a Concept is not scalable (such as for businesses like consulting or the performing arts – ones that depend on individual personalities).

The second Key requires understanding the **Business Model** itself. The Business Model for a scalable business may be very different than the Business Model with which you started. In order to continue to grow, you may have to change how you price, how you collect money, or introduce new products and services to offset instability in your cash flow.

A business without a sustainable Business Model will fail. This is true for start-up businesses as well as businesses that can use scale to continue to grow.

The third Key is the **Market**. This does not refer merely to having access to the market. A scalable company understands the market and automates; can message to it appropriately; knows how to build customer loyalty; and creates a platform for sustainable market growth. This platform is a multi-legged stool that projects an image of the business that is larger than it is in reality but to which it aspires.

The final Key to successfully scaling a business involves your business **Processes**. We'll discuss later the importance of Processes in lowering expenses in a growing business, but major Processes include: lead generation, marketing and sales execution, production of your product or service, and delivery of your product or service. These are the fundamental pieces that drive the growth of your company, and you need to deliver each of them more efficiently than you did previously, especially if your product or service taxes the efforts of your organization's ability to deliver on these different processes.

To summarize, the Four Keys to successfully scaling your business, regardless of size, are: Concept, Business Model, Market, and Processes.

## Principles of Scale Can Help Struggling Businesses

The concepts behind scaling your business don't apply only when you're big and successful. Even struggling businesses can use these four elements to boost sales and lower expenses. In many cases, struggling businesses suffer from the same fundamental problems experienced by businesses that are "maxed out" on their ability to deliver their product or service efficiently, such as my business's inability to take on more clients without cloning me.

Before we discuss how a large business can benefit from evaluating the principles of the Four Keys of Scale, let's discuss an example of how they can help a struggling business.

### Concept

One of the biggest challenges struggling businesses face is the lack of a clear Concept of what they offer. They may have created a high-quality product, but it's not something that people want to buy. Often, business owners feel so passionately about their product or service that they can't "hear the market" telling them that it doesn't want what they are selling. Even if a business has a product people want, the business may not be able to differentiate itself adequately from 'noise' in the market. Every business needs a Unique Selling Proposition (USP). The smaller the business, the more it needs a USP. Struggling operations cannot compete as "me too" businesses; they need to stake out a clear position and deliver value in a way that no one else can or does.

### Business Model

Many companies that fail blame the lack of capital. In reality, lack of capital is a symptom, not a cause of failure. A good Business Model requires figuring out how to generate cash quickly and consistently.

The siren song of venture capital has made many business owners think they need access to millions of dollars in order to build their businesses. While some Business Models, such as pharmaceuticals and technology hardware, require large investments of capital, most businesses don't need that. What they do need is a viable way of generating enough cash to sustain themselves.

## Market

Having access to a market means not just achieving market penetration, but having a message that resonates with your target consumer. Many businesses that can't get traction in the Market suffer from a lack of a well-defined Concept and target Market. When that Concept isn't clear, or when the business hasn't done the work to understand its customers' profiles, it will struggle. Such businesses often have an inadequate understanding of what resonates with their prospective customers. Doing the work to understand who buys and why will pay huge dividends in terms of shortening the sales cycle, building trust and loyalty, and increasing purchase volume.

## Processes

Where a business loses money, the Process is usually to blame. Companies need efficient and effective processes for marketing and sales automation, product manufacturing, and delivery in order to succeed.

It is usually not difficult to identify the problem in most businesses. If a business generates leads and cannot profitably convert those leads into customers, it may have a marketing automation problem. But if the business generates leads and cannot profitably deliver the product or service, then the problem may be in production.

If your business is struggling to achieve traction or profitability, evaluate your Four Keys to Scale: Concept, Business Model, Market, and Process. In order to transform your under-performing business into a sustainably profitable one, apply the Four Keys to Scale to break through the Growth Ceiling.

## Fire You!

When people ask me about the promises of having a scalable business, I tell them it's an opportunity to fire yourself. That's a concept that doesn't make a lot of sense to business owners, but fundamentally, it refers to the difference between having a *job* and having a *business*.

Most business owners did not start companies in order to create jobs for themselves. They wanted to build business assets, something they could pass on, something that gave them freedom, flexibility and autonomy, as opposed to a job – something one gets trapped in and stuck doing.

Before attempting to create scale, you need to think about the idea of firing yourself from your own business. How would your business operate tomorrow if you literally could not operate in it? If it fails without you, identify all the functions that would fail, from customer relations to sales to delivery. Those are the areas that need to change.

There are two fundamental truths one must face in order to understand what is necessary to scale:

1. Unless you make changes, your business will become more and more expensive to operate. Much like the concept of entropy in science, functions tend to become more chaotic when left to their own devices. They don't become ordered unless you exercise the effort to create that order.

2. The business you built is not the business you can grow, so your thinking must change. Your business must undergo a metamorphosis.

These two philosophical principles represent the underpinnings of this entire book. It is necessary to do things differently in order to grow our businesses. We need to fire ourselves to free up time to think strategically about the future, and run businesses instead of having jobs.

This is the promise I make to business owners who can face these two principles bravely: by applying the Four Keys to Scale, a business owner can create a business asset that he can pass on to others without needing to be involved in its operations on a day-to-day basis.

As we go through each of the chapters in this book, you will notice there are exercises. These are intended to facilitate your thinking about how to scale your business. *Don't skip past them.* Often, the exercises build upon each other and you cannot complete the exercise in a future chapter without doing the ones that preceded it.

Picking up this book defines you as an ambitious business owner, so you may be tempted to skip forward to what you have already identified as a source of difficulty. Please resist that temptation and follow the book in order. It's important to have the foundation of each of the core elements in order to succeed.

Another reason to proceed in order and perform all the exercises is that businesses often think they have a Process problem whereas they actually have a Concept problem. It's important to spend the time solidifying a Concept that is scalable and can be grown before trying to create Processes around something that cannot be scaled or is unable to grow.

As you complete these exercises, you'll notice that they are designed to change over time. As your business grows and expands, you'll reach new Growth Ceilings. When that happens, go back through these exercises again and figure out how to alleviate the pressure that is keeping you from growing to the next revenue stage.

Feedback is an important part of growing a business. It is necessary to listen to changing market demands and adjust your business trajectory accordingly. Business owners who are willing to take the courageous steps necessary to change the things about their business to allow scalable growth will experience the joy in being able to move from a job they've trapped themselves in to being engaged in a business they love.

Are you ready for the journey? Let's go.

# Chapter 2. What is Scale?

## To Scale is Human

What they don't tell you in business school is that human beings want to scale. What does that mean? It means that most people aren't happy remaining stuck in a static state. Business owners become entrepreneurs in order to see something grow or make something better; once a business gets into a position at which it can't grow any further, it is human nature to be dissatisfied with that state.

We all know stories of businesses that have decided they're big enough and decide not to grow any further, or didn't become any more than they were, but today's entrepreneurs are wired differently; they stretch themselves. They've entered the business world to create something for themselves and for others, and didn't want to be tied to a job.

As a business owner realizes that more and more of his time goes into service existing clients and has less and less time for family, friends, and hobbies, he becomes dissatisfied with the vision he had had when he first decided to go into business: he can't go on vacation, can't leave the business for any length of time: he always has to be "in touch." He is always "on duty."

As is commonly referred to as the "e-myth," many business owners start their business because they enjoy what they do; they are practitioners in their own business. But an entrepreneurial business owner creates an asset that he can pass on to somebody else. That means that the business must be structured in such a way that he can leave and it would still continue operating.

This is why corporate structures such as partnerships and corporations don't have expiration dates. Even after the original business owner is long gone, the entity can continue to function with other people in the original roles, or filling roles that didn't exist at the time that the business was created.

But even a potential business purchaser needs to see the Four Keys to Scale in place. The business needs to have a Concept that makes sense and that is unique. The Business Model must support long-term cash flow. The Market needs to be accessible and enable growth, and the Processes need to be in place so that the major functions that the original business owner had been fulfilling can continue to be fulfilled even without him.

We'll discuss each of these different Keys and how they work together to create a business asset, but you can imagine the difficulties that a business purchaser would have if he considers buying a business in which all the value, all the clients, and all of the leads are generated by the business owner's personal experience and intuition. You can't bottle that and pass it on.

If I can't replicate what you're doing, then what you're doing has no value for me as a buyer. This is the challenge that most business owners face.

## Why Can't You Just Grow As Is?

A lot of business owners think that in order to scale, all they need to do is keep doing what they're doing – just do more of it. For example, business owners of consulting businesses who find themselves "maxed out" and without any personal time may believe that if they keep hiring people, they'll grow a consulting company that becomes quite large.

If you think about it, there really aren't many large consulting firms. That's because consulting relies heavily on individuals' expertise and relationships in a manner that isn't directly scalable. The largest ones generally perform other tasks besides consulting. They may have started as tax and audit firm with a consulting arm, then decided to separate the tax and audit portion of the business from the consulting portion, which may be quite large. But this model is the exception and not the rule.

An analysis of small businesses throughout the United States found that consulting companies tend to reach a Growth Ceiling somewhere between two and five million dollars a year in revenue. The reason for this is marginal cost. Marginal cost is the additional cost that's required to deliver one more dollar of product or service. This is easy to understand if you produce physical goods; the marginal cost of delivering one more physical good is the cost of that good plus the cost of delivering that good. What's usually not included in marginal cost are concepts such as the investment to establish manufacturing facilities, or the cost of additional labor to support the facility.

The cost of labor or other resources to produce and deliver the product is part of marginal cost. These costs represents the variable portion of a company's expenses (they are variable because if sales decline, the additional employees who were hired to service the greater sales volume can be laid off to reduce a company's overall expenses).

In a consulting firm or any business that doesn't have scale, marginal cost is generally a problem. Either it's quite high, or it's out of control. In a consulting firm that has achieved scale, marginal cost is fairly flat; the amount of effort required to deliver a consulting hour is equal to the salary of the person who delivers that service, plus taxes and additional benefits. This doesn't change regardless of how many hours the person sells. If a salaried consultant works twenty hours a week, the marginal cost is the same per hour as if he works forty hours a week. If you hire more people, marginal cost doesn't change as these people are paid for the hours they work. Certainly, one can add junior staff (with lower billing rates) to consulting projects to achieve lower marginal costs, but this can only take you so far because staff that is billed on a consulting project is generally a high expense.

The challenge with consulting firms is actually much more insidious. Marginal costs do not really remain flat; they actually increase. That is because as the consulting company grows larger, it becomes more difficult to find new clients. It also becomes more difficult to hire and train qualified staff. Although creating processes for consulting projects is possible and allows projects to be delivered more quickly, most consulting firms have revenue models that are proportionate to the amount of hours spent on delivering the project. Even those consulting firms that offer fixed pricing can get caught in this trap. The scale that you would think could be achieved by collecting additional overhead dollars from all these projects gets eaten up in a bureaucracy that is top-heavy and is difficult to keep retained, happy, and effective.

This is why consulting companies don't typically grow very large: the more product you deliver, the more expensive it becomes to deliver. Larger consulting companies charge higher rates, but there is a natural ceiling at which a customer is willing to pay for consulting services. Any new, smaller, more agile, and therefore cheaper, consulting company that can deliver the same quality service at a lower cost is at an advantage. This creates a drag on the large consulting company's growth and causes it to stagnate.

You may not have created a consulting company, but you may still be dealing with a similar problem of scale. Instead of billing each person by the hour, you may find that the difficulty of keeping track of production keeps you from lowering your marginal costs on an ongoing basis. Your marginal cost may be flat or actually increasing just like the typical consulting firms. Or you might be a solopreneur who is doing all the work and whose time is maxed out, in which case the marginal cost is infinite because you simply don't have any more time to give.

These are situations that cause companies to stop growing, and companies that can't grow either stagnate or start to shrink. As there is always competition in the marketplace, your company cannot expect to keep doing what it has been doing and expect that its revenues and profits will remain stable. A company must move forward; if you're maxed out, you're only substituting one customer for another one. It is like treading water: a lot of work, exhausting, and you typically don't get anywhere.

Much like the amount of energy needed to launch a rocket must remain steady until the rocket reaches a certain altitude, if the engine cuts out too soon, the rocket will plummet back to earth. Like that rocket, your company needs engines to propel it past the pull of gravity so that it can continue on its growth trajectory. Scale is what fuels that trajectory.

## The Goal: Decreasing Marginal Costs

How do we solve this problem of increasing marginal costs accompanying growth? The goal behind scaling your company is to *decrease* marginal costs. A company that is perfectly scaled is one in which the marginal cost of delivering each new product is either zero or close to zero.

If you think about companies that have achieved scale, such as companies that deliver digital products that involve no human intervention, the marginal cost is nearly zero. The bandwidth necessary to deliver a digital product to a new customer is negligible in comparison to a business's other expenses. Therefore, it can add an almost infinite number of customers because the cost associated with the increase in sales isn't outpaced by the growth and revenue.

In order to purchase this kind of market share, the company can even afford to *lower* prices to eliminate competition with inefficient business models. As scale increases, the company can decrease prices because the volume generated at a lower price often exceeds the lower volume sold at a higher price with a lower market reach. That's how scaled companies drive unscaled companies out of business.

Of course, it clearly costs money to acquire new customers, so it's important to understand what automation and processes are in place in order to generate new leads and convert them into customers. As companies adopt marketing and sales automation, they're able to decrease the cost of client of lead generation and client acquisition. As these costs decrease and delivery costs remain low, the company is able to be at scale. However when human beings are involved, there is clearly a non-trivial marginal cost component.

How do these principles apply to you if you're a consulting firm? Such firms have to do something very different to decrease marginal costs. That means automating delivery of a product as well as automating some of the marketing and sales functions. This seems counterintuitive and will require, essentially, a different product than what the company had been delivering in the past, but this is unavoidable.

A company that delivers expensive, high marginal cost products and services must develop something new and innovative in order to scale their Business Model. It is not possible to keep "high touch" (those involving human interaction) products and services as the primary source of income in a company that chooses to scale without developing appropriate automation.

This requires "productizing" your company. We'll discuss different ways to develop product in Chapter 17 but for now it is important to understand that the product or service you're delivering today may not be the product or service that you can deliver into the future. This requires changing your Business Model. It may even require you to change the Concept on which your entire business is based, but these are the kinds of pivots that businesses need to adopt and execute in order to remain viable as they grow.

As we proceed through the sections that follow, we'll address each of the Keys to Scale that are necessary for your business to decrease marginal costs. Keep in mind how your business performs the different functions we discuss so you can see how today's version of events needs to change to become one that, as you add additional people, makes it easier to execute the Process.

The cornerstone of the concept of Scale that is important to understand and remember is the following: as you do something more frequently, it must become easier and less expensive to do so.

# Section 2. The Concept

# Chapter 3. The Offer

## Target Market

As I mentioned earlier, most companies can see huge lift in sales by focusing on a niche. As it's often said: "Get Niche. Get Rich."

But let's dig down to understand why it's so important to have a well-defined target market.

Clearly identifying your target market accomplishes three things for you, all having to do with focus. First, it focuses your *thinking* on a small group of prospects. Second, it focuses your *advertising* on places where your prospects are likely to be found. And third, it focuses your *product* on solving one particular problem.

Let's look at each benefit separately. When you focus your thinking around a small group of prospects, you get to know them. By this I mean you get inside the mind, the psyche, of your potential customers. You can dissect what they need, what they worry about, what they want to hear. We'll delve deeper into this in Chapter 4, but for now what's important to know that we cannot do this for one hundred different kinds of customers, but you can do it for five or six – ten at most.

I advise my clients to limit their focus to a target market so they can better address that market. Think about how you would react. Imagine you were a small business owner who sells to retail stores. If your business were being solicited by two well-qualified service providers: one that specializes in businesses that sell to retail, and one that does not. Which would you choose to be your service provider?

You might be asking yourself: "Won't I miss out on some business by being so focused?"

Yes, you will, but most business owners report that by having a well-defined target market, you'll pick up business that you're currently not getting. And since you're focused on that market, not only will you be likely to convert a higher percentage of your prospective customers, but you'll be able to charge more for your services. In other words, you'll gain far more than you'll lose.

The second benefit comes when it's time to advertise. Having a focused target market helps you identify where your prospects "hang out." Are they looking for your services online or offline? Do they use social media? Do they follow bloggers or media personalities? Do they belong to specific associations or groups?

I tell my clients that if they can't identify where their target market spends their time, then their target market is probably too broad. A well-focused target market is part of a community; as a service provider, you need to become a part of that community, too.

Belonging takes time and effort in order to be viewed as a value-added member of that community. You can't do that for ten or twenty different communities at the same time. You don't have time to focus on every customer and every market. You need to be selective.

The third benefit has to do with creating or defining a product that will offers benefits to your target market and is cost-effective to create and offer. One common problem companies often have is that their product is so "multi-featured" that no one really knows what it does. Because the founder and/or product designer wanted to make sure that their product "covered all the bases," they built in bells and whistles that may not be needed. These "features" don't add value but only confuse the message.

By focusing on a target market, you can easily filter your product features according to the functions they fulfill. If your target market doesn't need that feature, it shouldn't be part of the product.

Similarly, you can package features that would be uniquely interesting to your target market in ways that create new product.

It's critical to design a Minimum Viable Solution, both when you start out and when you relaunch your product. When sales lag and you need to reposition your product, you need to throw the dead weight overboard. Having a well-defined target market will help you differentiate the dead weight from the critical cargo.

What if your target market is too narrow? When my clients ask this question, I'm usually pretty skeptical; I rarely see a target market that is too narrowly defined. But it's certainly possible to define a market so narrowly that you can't find prospects. That happens if you only have one or two types of customer profiles and they're very specific. This is rarely the problem; the opposite is more often the case.

For now, let's assume that your target market is not too narrowly defined, and when we develop customer profiles in Chapter 4, we'll test this assumption. You can always reevaluate the market and broaden it, if necessary, but usually the danger is having a market that's defined too broadly rather than the other way around.

## One Big Problem

Many of my clients tell me their product solves many big problems. That's a serious complication. Often the reason a product doesn't sell is because it's not clear what problem it solves. Much like the exercise of defining the target market, we'll now go through an exercise in focusing on the one major problem your product (and this applies if your product is a service, too) solves.

Why narrow the benefit? Just as in defining your target market, focusing on what problem your product solves will help you focus your marketing message. It will also help focus your product development efforts and your sales execution.

A common objection I hear is that focusing on One Big Problem leaves money on the table. When your sales are down and your product has no traction, there is *no* money on the table to be had. You need to concentrate on building a business around one success. After that, you can branch out into other areas. As long as your target market is large enough and their One Big Problem is common enough, you're in business.

Think about your most successful client. If you don't have a client yet, think about your ideal client. Picture a profitable, happy customer.

What sales message resonated with this client? Which components of your product did they use and which did they not use? What was their Pain Point (the problem they need to solve)? What story would they tell about the problem you solved for them?

All of these questions help identify the One Big Problem that your product solves.

How can you tell if your target One Big Problem is common enough to build a business around? Simple: Google it. This is a good test to see if you can articulate your problem. If you can't define it for a Google search, you haven't thought enough about the core problem you're solving.

Try Googling different variations of the One Big Problem that your product solves and see what's written on the subject. Use Google's search filters to limit results to the past year. Review the articles on the first two pages of listings. You should see two types of listings for the One Big Problem: blog posts or articles, and ads or offers to solve the problem.

First, you should see blog posts or articles written about the problem. Perhaps they just identify the fact that it is a problem, or perhaps they propose solutions. It doesn't matter what type of entries these are or who is writing about the subject as long as the problem is occurring presently.

Next, you should see some service providers offering solutions to the One Big Problem. If there are no service providers, that could be a bad sign. Many entrepreneurs think that having no competition is a good thing, but that is rarely the case. It might mean that the market for solving the problem hasn't yet been validated or recognized. You need some competition to validate the market. Competition means that the problem is recognized and that people are being paid to solve it.

It's like being a pioneer in the Old West. The pioneer, the one who first defines and creates the market, tends to be the one who gets arrows in his back. For that reason, it's usually better *not* to be the first in the market but to let someone else do the hard work of defining the problem to the market.

Say your product helps drive traffic to a client's website. Run a Google search on "getting traffic for your website" Some examples from the first few pages are:

"Generating traffic without Google" (so you don't need search engine optimization); "Boosting traffic for free" (so you don't have to pay someone or buy some product to drive traffic for you); and "How to increase traffic without marketing" (to generate passive traffic without active promotion). The fact that you find many hits like these suggests that there is a market interested in finding new ways to drive traffic to websites, and if you have a product that does it more efficiently, less expensively, or in a different (but believable) way than your competition, there is a market for it.

If you don't find Google entries on a problem or solutions for it, or if you only find a few but not enough to fill up two pages of listings, there are two things you might want to do: either abandon the problem and think of another problem you can solve, or expand the definition of the problem.

Expanding the definition of the problem means expanding some of the limitations you may have put on your description of your product. For example, maybe the problem you seek to solve focuses on document retention for small offices. You can expand that problem statement by looking at document retention for all offices, not just small ones.

You can also expand the definition of the problem by looking at parallel problems – ones that occur at the same time as the one you seek to address. For example, if the One Big Problem is document retention for offices, you can expand the problem by looking not just as document retention, but include searching document archives. This problem is related and parallel to document retention. You preserve documents so you can search for them.

This solution also works if your One Big Problem is not big enough. You can broaden it by thinking about why it's important for your target market to solve that problem.

To accomplish this, use the "5 Whys" technique. When you state how important it is to solve the problem, ask "why" it's important. When you answer the question, ask "why," again. Ask "why" five times until you've uncovered either the real problem or have identified enough parallel problems to expand your One Big Problem.

Let's say that the service you sell is helping companies create videos, and you want to convince your customer to invest in creating quality video assets. Here's an example of a statement of how important it is to solve the problem, and how to apply the "5 Whys."


**"It's important to create good quality video for your business."**

*Why* do you need quality video?

"Because quality video shows you are serious about what you do."

*Why* do you need to be serious to get work?

"Because if you're serious, you will invest in your business."

*Why* do you need to hire someone who is investing in their business?

"Because otherwise they may just be a beginner."

**_Why_ can't you be a beginner?**

"Because beginners aren't experts."

**_Why_ do you need to be an expert?**

"Because experts get paid more."

Ah, so you're not helping people create quality video assets; you're helping them _increase their income_.

## One Big Result

Now we come to the most critical part of your product positioning: your One Big Result.

Like our previous conversations, many companies say, "But our product has more than One Big Result." Maybe, but if you can't identify the one "big one," you will have a difficult time engaging your customer in a dialog about how you can help them solve the One Big Problem you identified in the last section.

If you've done the work to identify the One Big Problem you solve, then your One Big Result should be an extension of that. But before giving your knee-jerk reaction to answer this question, let's think about the language of benefits.

Your customers think in terms of their own language, their industry's own jargon. The biggest mistake most companies make in messaging is using their own language or jargon to describe the One Big Result.

For example, one software company I worked with provided pricing analytics. Their initial One Big Result was "optimal pricing." Well, no one really understands what that means. Optimal pricing was what they provided, but the One Big Result actually _derived from_ optimal pricing: it was higher profit.

You should think about that Concept, as well. What would your customer explain to the CEO or the Board about why these needed to buy the product? What one sentence wraps up your Value Proposition?

If you break it down to basics, there are very few things that customers do: they earn money, they save money, they stay out of jail (comply with regulation and law), and they feel better about themselves. That's pretty much it. You should cast your One Big Result in those terms. When you understand these customer needs, you'll be closer to understanding the One Big Result you offer your customers. I call that the Main Benefit.

But knowing the Main Benefit is just the first step. Your customer can earn money or save money a lot of different ways. And of course, they can do it the hard way. Your job is to help them do it the easy way – by offering techniques to accomplish the job more quickly or efficiently: changes that your client can believe in. That means your One Big Result needs to help them achieve higher revenues or cost savings (or whatever) *while simultaneously* controlling something else.

For example, your One Big Result might be: "We help you increase your revenue while lowering your process costs." The "This While That" formula is a powerful way of making your One Big Result much more impressive. Think about your product and how it helps achieve the Main Benefit while keeping something else in check. That second part is what I call the Controlling Factor.

There are a number of different things you can control. You can control costs; you can control the time frame by which something occurs; and you can control the state of mind of your customer. These give you many ways of increasing the value of the Main Benefit you offer. It's one thing to make more money but it's something entirely different to make more money *while* saving money.

So your One Big Result needs to be expressed as a Main Benefit with a *while* Controlling Factor. Of course, there are many ways of saying the same thing: "This and That" or "This but That" or even "This with

That." But any way you say it, your One Big Result starts with a Main Benefit and ends with a Controlling Factor.

Here are a few examples:

"We increase sales by 23% while shortening your sales cycle." [*Revenue controlling time*]

"We save you 15% on the cost of food while improving the quality of your end product." [*Cost controlling quality.*]

"We keep you in compliance with government regulations while improving the productivity of your staff by 21%." [*Compliance controlling cost.*]

One last point before you write your own One Big Result. You want this One Big Result to be something no one else can say. Many times we identify a unique Value Proposition that isn't really unique. You might offer great quality or have a great team. Everyone can say that. Even if they're lying, your competition can probably say many of the same things you say and get away with it.

Your One Big Result must be something no one else can say and be credible. That's why specificity with the use of numbers is so helpful. If you can quote a statistic as part of your One Big Result, you're in great shape. Specificity adds credibility to your message.

But one thing about statistics: don't round them up or down. If you save people an average of 23%, say "23%;" don't round down to 20% or up to 25%. Psychologists have shown that unusual numbers (like "23") carry more credibility with the listener. It makes it seem like you didn't just "make it up."

It also adds uniqueness to your message. Your competition might repeat your line about cost savings or high quality, but they are unlikely to copy your statistics.

Come up with your own One Big Result by thinking carefully about your target market and the One Big Problem you solve.

## EXERCISE 3.1 YOUR TARGET MARKET

Develop your focused target market.

1. Are you focusing on consumers or businesses? _____

_____

2. Describe the demographics of your customer (e.g. if they are a consumer: income, location, age, family status, interests, etc. If they are a business: revenue, location, industry vertical, maturity, etc.)

_____

_____

_____

_____

_____

_____

## EXERCISE 3.2 YOUR ONE BIG PROBLEM

1. State your One Big Problem: _____

2. Do the Google search we described. What comes up in the first two pages of the search?

3. If you have to expand your problem statement, because it's not a "big enough" problem, use the "5 Whys." Why is it important for your target market to solve this problem? _____

3a. Why is that the case? _____

3b. Why is that the case? _____

3c. Why is that the case? _____

3d. Why is that the case? _____

4. Restate your final "One Big Problem" by expanding your original problem statement: _____

## EXERCISE 3.3 YOUR ONE BIG RESULT

1. Describe your main benefit (hint: it's usually revenue, costs, compliance, or quality of life.) _____

_____

_____

2. Identify the top 3 factors you can control: (hint: cost, quality, time, productivity, compliance, quality of life, state of mind, etc.)

_____

_____

_____

3. Choose your one big result by using the formula "Main Benefit *While* Controlling Factor." Feel free to change "while" to "and," "but," or "with" if it makes more sense. _____

_____

_____

# Chapter 4. The Customer

## Identifying Your Customer Profile

The most important part of communicating with your audience is knowing who your audience is. Unfortunately, most companies stop at defining their target market and never get more specific. It's not enough to understand the characteristics of your buyers in broad terms; you need to know them personally and individually.

People buy from people. You need to understand the people, the human element, you're selling to. If your prospects are a faceless, nameless set of pre-qualification questions, you'll miss the number one reason people buy: to fulfill a true, human need.

The best way to understand your audience is by defining it, personally. A customer profile is a powerful tool to help personalize your messaging. Even a narrow target market may have several customer profiles. You need to develop their profiles and understand them before you can start marketing and selling to them.

A customer profile consists of two parts: demographics and psychographics. Demographics represent the characteristics that describe the person you're selling to. Psychographics, a term that may be unfamiliar, represents the opinions, lifestyles, and behaviors of that individual. Psychographics are sometimes more important than demographics.

In order to develop customer profiles, we're going to identify five to ten key customer types and write down the demographics and psychographics of each one. We're going to get personal, naming each individual corresponding to the profile. Of course, each profile is simply a "stand-in" for a group of prospects, but we should be as descriptive as possible.

One caution for companies that sell to businesses: we often think that, since we sell to businesses, the business is the profile. This can be a costly mistake. Just because we sell to a business doesn't mean that the person we sell to doesn't matter.

Sometimes we call this "Role-Based Selling" in a corporate environment, but in the end, the person who buys from us has individual needs: to increase success, reduce stress, become a hero, get a bonus, etc. If we can't identify those needs, we will not be able to connect with that individual on a personal enough level to make a trusted offer of our product or service.

## Customer Demographics

The first part of each customer profile should be a list of the profile demographics. I will list a starter set of demographics that you should write down. Remember: we're trying to tell a story with each profile. Imagine a real person sitting in front of you as you write this down. The more personal – the more human – the better.

This list should, by no means, be considered exhaustive. If you can define more than I ask, you should do so.

Name: Don't skip this. Give this potential customer a name. Choose a name and gender so you can focus on who you're selling to. The name personalizes the rest of the profile. More than that, though, it serves as a moniker for the profile that you can share with others. It's a shortcut communication vehicle that helps keep everyone's mind on the person to whom you're offering a solution.

Age: It's okay to give a range, but try not to use too broad a range, such as 18-55. Even if you offer your product to multiple categories of people, try to split them up by age band. You'll be surprised to see how different their needs are and, therefore, you need to modify your messaging to different age ranges.

Income: Take a stab at identifying an income range. Even if income isn't specifically related to your product, knowing the typical range of income is part of knowing your prospect's phase of life.

Family status: You might think that these kinds of personal details don't matter, but they do. Family status can often provide you with insight into some of the 'soft' benefits your product offers, whether you're selling to a consumer or a business buyer. Prospects that are married or in committed relationships often respond favorably to messages about gaining more free time or becoming more efficient at their jobs. Prospects who are single often respond favorably to messages about upward mobility and achievement.

Obviously, this is not an exhaustive list, but having a framework for your marketing messaging can be a very powerful way of connecting with the unspoken needs and desires of your prospect.

If you believe your prospect has children, come up with a number of children, their ages, and maybe even their names. Sure, it's not accurate, but it personalizes your prospect even more and helps you "get inside their head."

If you think your prospect may be divorced or recently separated from a significant other, this can also be a powerful detail. The psychological needs of the prospect will be powerful and important. For example, a recently divorced buyer may feel a need for acceptance. Ignore them at your own financial peril.

Wage earning status: Is your prospect solely responsible for providing for themselves and their family? Does he or she share that responsibility with someone else? Is your prospect dependent upon someone else to provide for his or her financial needs?

Geographic location: Be as specific as you can about where your prospect lives. The kind of geography that matters depends, of course, on your product. Geography, however, is a powerful dividing line that can give you great insight into different messages.

For example, for some companies, broad geography, such as region of the country or city, are very important because they indicate different spending trends or social norms. However, geography could be more descriptive: urban, suburban, or rural. The more descriptive geographic demographics tie different regions of the country together into like group that, while separated by long distances, actually behave similarly and may even share core needs and wants.

<u>Residence type</u>: Don't laugh. Think house, condo, or apartment. The home life of the prospect is critical to understanding their needs. Even if their living situation is not directly related to your product, understanding what they consider "comfortable" is critical.

There are many other customer demographics you can consider. You may think you're just "guessing." That's okay. The thought process is a useful exercise. Obviously, your prospects will be different and fall along a spectrum of these characteristics. You can adjust your messaging as necessary. But without a clear understanding of what a "typical" prospect may look like, you will not be able to connect with them on an emotional level. That emotional connection will propel your marketing and sales efforts.

## Customer Psychographics

More powerful than demographics, psychographics are the key to understanding the needs and desires of your prospect. We'll go through a list of several important characteristics, but they are by no means the only ones you should think about.

Use what you know about a prospect's demographics to help craft their personal psychographics. It's important to be as specific as you can be. If you find that a similar demographic profile may have vastly different psychographic profiles, split them up into separate customer profiles (with different names.) Feel free to add to this list as it applies to your product.

Interests and hobbies: What your prospect does in their free time can play an important role in your messaging. Don't be lazy about identifying this, such as assuming that football is a hobby because you happen to see a trophy or plaque on your prospect's wall. Interests tell you a story about what the prospect values. Are they a team sports player? Do they like to travel or do things that are adventurous? Do they stick pretty close to home and "play it safe?" Is family important?

Each of these questions as indicated by a list of interests helps you develop a picture of who your audience really is.

Personal goals: Make a list of three personal goals for your prospect. Some goals may be stated while some may be more personal. By understanding your prospect's goals, you will understand better how you will help your prospect achieve them or, in some cases, how your product might make achieving some of their goals more difficult.

For example, automating your prospect's main function in their office may make it more difficult for them to get promoted because they have fewer opportunities to shine. Knowing that your product could be an obstacle for your prospect is a critical piece of information, too. It will help you anticipate objections, both stated and unstated. Once you know your prospect's goals, you should try to align a benefit with their goals.

Frustrations: These may or may not be related to the prospect's personal goals. List three or four of your prospect's frustrations. What keeps them up at night? When they daydream, what kinds of problems do they wish would go away? What bugs them about their job or their life?

Fears: Name two or three things that your prospect fears. They may be related to the One Big Problem you're solving, or they may be related to their job or family or financial situation. Even if they aren't directly related to their jobs, understanding the fears that motivate your prospect will help you craft the correct messaging. The more you can allay their fears through your product's benefits, either directly or indirectly, the more you will connect on a human level with your prospect. This connection will allow you to build a deeper relationship of trust – trust that will be critical to your ability to sell.

Objections: If they hear about your product, what will their objections be? What are their concerns? What would they tell you to your face? What would they say behind your back to others or to their boss?

This part of the exercise can be the most difficult because it requires some serious honesty with yourself. In my experience, most companies are afraid to verbalize the real objections to their products because they may identify a gap or flaw in the product or service. But this is the time to do it. You can fix that gap later, but if you can't admit to yourself that there are honest objections, you'll be blindsided by them in the field.

So don't be lazy and just come up with the "easy" objections, such as price. Think hard about what your competitors say about you, and what keeps people from buying your product.

Buying trigger: The one, silver-bullet sentence that, when your prospect hears it (and assuming they believe it), will cause them to make the decision to buy your product. I think this is the most important element of the customer profile. It helps you coalesce all of this work into a core message that will focus your sales and marketing efforts. There are no "magic words" to include in your phrase to make your prospect buy. First you have to earn their trust, credibility, and respect. But eventually, you have to convince your prospect that your silver-bullet sentence is true, unique to your product, and can't be stated by your competition.

## How Many Profiles Are Too Many? (Or Too Few?)

The exercise you have just completed is not a one-time event. Your target market should consist of between five and ten of these distinct customer profiles that differ from each other in significant ways. In other words, don't just change the person's name and age.

You can differentiate between significantly different customer profiles by looking at their goals, objections, and buying triggers. Of course, the demographics are important too, but demographics generally serve to shape the psychographics, not the other way around.

Take the time to craft five to ten really clear and different customer profiles within the target market you've chosen.

It can be tempting to let this exercise run away with you a bit. Focus on five or ten profiles. If you find that there are truly more than ten distinctly different profiles in your target market, consider narrowing the market. You will not be able to effectively message to so many distinct customer types in a single campaign.

That's not to say that your product or service can't have applicability across more than ten different customer profiles, but if you're having difficulty gaining traction, you will have to focus. Spreading your marketing messages too thinly (to include many different customer profiles) will not get you the traction you need.

On the other hand, if you're having difficulty finding more than two or three different profiles, then you might think about widening your target market as I discussed in the previous chapter. It is rare for a viable target market to be very narrow.

I challenge my clients to think more creatively about the types of profiles in their target market to expand the list to at least five profiles. Sometimes, though, there really isn't that much variation and it is beneficial to target more broadly.

## B2C and B2B Examples

Let's take two examples: B2C (business-to-consumer) and B2B (business-to-business).

B2C: Let's consider, as an example, a personal trainer who sells one-on-one training services to busy female professionals. Before this exercise, the business Value Proposition was simply, "Exercise on Your Schedule." See how we re-position this Value Proposition based on a client profile.

Client profile for a personal trainer business:

Denise, age 30-55, income $100k-$150k annually, married, with children. She provides about half of the family income along with her husband. She has two children, both teenaged. She lives in a larger home in the suburbs and commutes into the city to work. She has a generally happy marriage, but both she and her spouse are quite busy and, because of their separate work schedules, she feels that they don't share a lot of time together anymore.

Her goals are to lose between ten and fifteen pounds. She wants to live a healthy lifestyle so that, as she ages, she doesn't become saddled with significant health issues. She has regular checkups, but doesn't always take as much time for her health as she would like. She's a bit embarrassed about that, but doesn't really know what to do about it. She wants to feel better about what she is doing for her health.

She's frustrated about the lack of time. She isn't able to spend as much time with her family as she would like. She's also frustrated because she knows what she needs to do but doesn't think she has time to do it. She used to exercise and manage her diet, but now, with late dinners at work and no time with the family, she believes that it's impossible to get in shape.

Her objections are going to be: "I don't have time;" "If I have to choose between spending time with my family or on myself, I'm going to choose my family;" and "I think I can manage by just eating a little less and get my exercise by taking the stairs a few times a week."

Her buying trigger is: "This means of getting you into shape will fit into your existing schedule and take no time away from your other priorities."

Look at how a subtle change in our messaging will hit the "hot button" for Denise. Instead of simply saying "on your schedule," we focus on not making her choose between her health and her family. This is a powerful repositioning of the service. If we gain Denise's trust by validating her concerns, she will believe the Value Proposition and we'll gain Denise as a client.

B2B: This business sells document retention software to law firms. Although one of the partners will sign off on the purchase, the Buyer is really the chief paralegal. Before this exercise, the message was, "Save Time and be More Efficient with our Software." Let's see how developing a client profile will help us reposition this.

Client profile for legal document retention software.

Mark, age 20-35, income $75k-$100k annually, single and dating. He is self-sufficient, in a growing career, and is upwardly mobile. He spends a great deal of time at work, and his social life is relegated to late nights and weekends. He lives in an apartment in the city very close to the office so he can and come and go as necessary. He's pretty happy with his career, but truth be told, he spends a lot of time with documents and doesn't find the work particularly fulfilling. It also doesn't win him any accolades at work; it's just boring. He'd love to have more time with his girlfriend.

His goals are to advance at work and earn a promotion to a job that would pay him more. With a promotion would come the chance to bring on staff to handle more of the administrative tasks that he dislikes. That would provide him with more time to have a life, and also more time to devote to more interesting work.

He's frustrated that his work is becoming more and more tedious. And in a firm where you're judged by your latest accomplishment, he can't be noticed if he's buried in paperwork. He's also frustrated in his relationship with his girlfriend; he's worried if he can't spend more time with her, she'll think that he doesn't care about her. They have had a few fights about that recently.

When you offer him a solution to his problem his objections are: "This is just more stuff for me to learn;" "We have a process for doing that, already;" and "If I ask them to buy this for me and it doesn't work, I'll look like a failure." Notice how this last objection will not be one that Mark will tell you explicitly.

His buying trigger is: "This solution will buy you time to do work that will really get you noticed as the hero."

Again, it's not a wholesale change of the Value Proposition, but a slight repositioning. But since it's repositioned to the real need of this client profile, you're in a much better position to get Mark's attention and business.

## EXERCISE 4.1 WRITE 5-10 OF YOUR OWN CUSTOMER PROFILES. DON'T SKIP THIS EXERCISE OR DO JUST ONE. SPEND THE TIME TO WRITE DOWN ENOUGH TO GET THE HANG OF IT.

### Demographics

Name: _____

Gender: _____ Age: _____ Income: _____

Family status: _____

Wage earning status: _____

Geographic location or type: _____

Residence type: _____

### Psychographics

List 3 personal goals:

1. _____

2. _____

3. _____

List up to 3 frustrations:

1. _____

2. _____

3. _____

List up to 5 fears:

1. _____

2. _____

3. _____

4. _____

5. _____

List up to 3 objections:

1. _____

2. _____

3. _____


Write this profile's buying trigger: _____
_____
_____

# Chapter 5. Audience Segments

## What is a "Need Segment?"

The migration path is all about how the prospect goes from being a potential customer to an actual customer. It refers to the fact that every prospect we meet is going to be different in some way. We have to treat people differently based upon their differing needs and where they are in the sales cycle, but first of all we need to identify who they are and what they want.

This means that if a customer is going to increase their interaction with you, going from being a prospect to becoming a customer, they are doing so on their own accord, or in other words, they are self-migrating. There's nothing that you're able to do to force them to move closer to you or move more quickly. That's why it is therefore important to keep in mind what motivates a prospect to move closer to you – closer to buying.

The first thing you'll notice is that our approach is radically different from the typical sales funnel which focuses on customers dropping down through the funnel. People don't drop through a sales funnel, and they don't, simply by gravity, move closer you.

We think it's far more accurate to visualize them moving up a ladder toward you. This also reflects the fact that energy needs to be expended to get a prospect to move up.

To show this energy, we have used colors to identify this process, starting from red all the way through to green as they move through the various stages.

*Figure 1. Four Prospect Need Segments*

These colors and the terms used are going to become very symbolic and are important in identifying the level of each customer that you're talking to. You need to pay careful attention to what is happening here.

When we deal with a prospect and they become someone who buys from us, they move through a certain number of stages; you can think about this in a retail environment by considering your experience while out shopping.

## Loiterer

You see a store that you've never been in before, and linger outside as you window shop. Maybe you're in the mall looking at the sign trying to figure out who the business is and what do they do.

Before you've even made the choice to engage at the level of looking at a particular business, you're basically *loitering*. It's a strong term, but it's a good one to explain that initial part of any interaction. This term applies to people who just come to your website and then pop right off again; the term 'high bounce rate' is used to describe these interactions.

Such individuals are Loiterers; they are not really prospects at this stage. They are people who are just coming to hang out, and so we assign this starting point a color: red.

The vast majority of people you come in contact with are Loiterers. You need a plan to deal with Loiterers in a way that quickly helps them find their way or identify with your target market. That's why defining target markets and customer profiles is so important. How can your prospect know if they're an ideal customer if you don't know, yourself?

## Looker

The next phase is the prospect being attracted to that business or moving toward the business in some way. This is the point at which you enter the store because you're just trying to get a sense of what's going on or what they sell.

We call that a Looker. Somebody who is just beginning to engage in your business, someone who doesn't know what's happening there yet, but is just *looking*. As this is a new stage, we have a new color to identify it: orange.

You know what this prospect is like. If you've ever been in a store approached by a salesperson you're not interested in talking to or wiling to engage with, what do you say? "I'm just *looking*." That's code for, "I'm not ready to tell you anything." That hesitancy is borne from lack of trust and lack of knowledge.

Many prospects don't want to share details about what they're thinking because they haven't developed a relationship of trust with you yet. They don't want to tell you what they need, or their fears, or what would help them succeed. Many salespeople find this out the hard way when they prematurely engage in aggressive questioning with prospects to qualify them or to try to discover their buying triggers. This usually results in making a Looker leave the store.

Before you can really make progress with a Looker, you're going to have to do some work. Specifically, you need to build trust and credibility. Until you can "get on the same side of the table" as your prospect, they will always view you as the "enemy." It's your job to change that perspective.

Often, though, a Looker can't tell you what they're looking for because they don't know yet. As a prospect starts to become familiar with what you offer, they are going to move through the phases of identifying some wants or preferences before they can pinpoint a specific need. Until they've identified that need, they're going to have a hard time explaining it to you.

That's why Lookers often need some time to browse, to develop trust and credibility. This is your opportunity to educate your audience. Then be ready to recognize the signs of migration – when a Looker moves to the next stage.

## Shopper

Now imagine that you're looking in this brand new store and suddenly something catches your eye. You realize that it's something you might want or need.

This would be the point at which you might pick up something from the shelf and examine it. At this point, you are comparing and contrasting. You look at the price, you look at the tag and you look at the product.

Now you're *shopping*: really engaged and ready to make a decision about whether this is something that you will buy. We also give that another color: yellow.

What you'll notice about very good shopkeepers or salespeople in retail stores is that they notice immediately when this change takes place. Lookers tend to wander the aisles – maybe not aimlessly, but without too much interest in any one particular thing. But a Shopper starts to inspect.

The salesperson that was previously told "I'm just looking" now approaches the Shopper with new interest. A good salesperson engages directly in the shopping experience, itself, with a comment like, "That would look good on you," or "That's one of our biggest sellers."

The trick is for you to notice this change among your prospects, even if you can't observe their behavior in real time. We'll spend some time talking about these migration signals and how to notice them in your own sales process. But for now, it's critical to recognize that there is a transition, and it's your job to notice it.

## Buyer

If the decision to purchase is positive, you move from being a Shopper to a Buyer. A Buyer is somebody who's ready to make a purchase. The color, of course, changes again: green.

A Buyer wants to transact business, and you need to make it easy for them to do so. A common mistake many salespeople make is slowing down the transaction process. Perhaps they underestimate the Buyer's desire to "close the deal" or perhaps they have a misguided concept of "up-selling."

In a retail environment, when a Shopper says they're ready to buy, a good salesperson often will acknowledge that desire and begin the process. They may still try to up-sell, but up-selling will become part of the transaction rather than a hurdle in the way of the transaction.

That distinction is important.

I'm sure you've had the experience of wandering around a department store trying to find the cash register or someone to run it. Some businesses create that same experience without even knowing it.

Knowing when someone is truly a Buyer and communicating the transaction process to them – especially when it's unfamiliar – is a critical part of your sales and marketing messaging, even if you don't think of it as such.

## *Customer*

Once a prospect completes the purchase transaction, they become a Customer. Many businesses view prospects and Customers as fundamentally different animals. I disagree.

Customers are prospects, too. We all know the adage that it's easier to get an existing customer to buy again then it is to get a new prospect to buy the first time. That means we handle Customers using the same marketing framework with which we handle prospects.

But their needs have changed. Because they purchased a product, their needs revolve around achieving the promised Value Proposition. They need information, service, and support. Assign the Customer a color: blue.

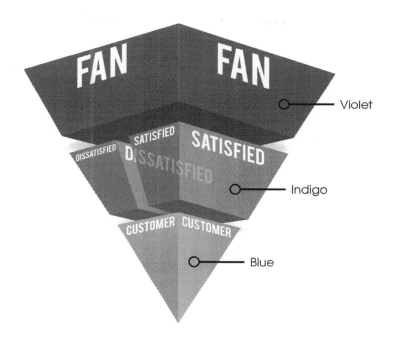

*Figure 2. Customer Need Segments*

Information to Customers is intended to inform them about the transaction. Your Customers need a receipt of the transaction, an understanding of payment terms, and, in the case of a more complex sale, such as a multi-million dollar business contract, instructions on how to navigate the accounting process with your company.

This information can be presented a number of different ways. Many businesses choose to present this information online. Some deliver it through direct contact with a sales or account executive.

In large ticket sales, it's always a good idea to have a long-term account executive whose job is to represent the company to the Customer. You will have a brief "honeymoon" period during which the Customer is happy with their purchase decision, but it doesn't take long for "Buyer's remorse" to creep in. The period immediately following the sale is a critical time to provide contact. Generally speaking, the more contact, the lower the likelihood of "Buyer's remorse," which leads to returns and refunds, or worse: dissatisfied customers and bad reviews.

After information about the transaction has been made available, the focus shifts to Service and Support. Although many people think these two concepts are interchangeable, they actually have very different purposes.

Service is what your company provides to assist your Customer when something goes wrong. Support is what your company provides to help your Customer use the product or service you sold them. You need both functions in your organization.

Don't confuse Service with "services." Your services may be additional products that are revenue-generating and provide support. But right now, I want to separate the revenue-generating products from what you offer to your Customer along with their purchase.

Your organization has the responsibility to communicate the Information, Service, and Support to your customer. This communication enables your customer to achieve that One Big Result you promised during the sales process. If you achieve it, they'll be generally satisfied. If not, they won't be, and you'll need to respond to that.

Customers fall into two major groups: satisfied and dissatisfied. The problem is, at any one moment, you don't know who is in which category for 80% of your customer base. That's usually because you don't ask.

Follow-up Information, Service, and Support with a Customer satisfaction survey. Make sure it's timed well. You don't want to survey too early and you don't want to survey too long after a critical interaction has passed.

Many organizations today make the mistake of over-surveying. This cheapens the value of the feedback. Collecting surveys on every single interaction with the Customer is a bad idea. Not every interaction is equal. Your organization may want to collect quality scores on your call center associates or customer service representatives, but badgering customers to rate every single interaction is bad practice – and yields bad statistics.

Pick the most critical interactions between you and your Customers. I work with my clients to identify the key "moments that matter." Survey immediately after those and on no other occasions. That will give you a true, stable, and meaningful sense of the mind of your customer.

And when they're unhappy, it's time to engage the full force of diplomacy to salvage the relationship. As with all diplomats, their efforts are in proportion to the value of the relationship. If you don't know the value, you can't successfully decide the best course of correction needed.

Once you have a truly satisfied Customer, even if they were recovered from an unsatisfactory experience, you have built a fan.

## Fan

A Fan is your biggest asset. A Customer becomes a Fan when they begin to engage in the revenue-generating process. The Fan gets assigned a color, too: purple.

Fans generate revenues in a number of ways, both direct and indirect. Here are some examples:

A customer refers new business

A customer buys more product

A customer offers a testimonial

A customer shares their positive experience with others

A customer provides vital feedback that improves your product offering.

In all of these cases, the Customer has become an arm of your sales and marketing team. They should be rewarded as such.

If you haven't created a formal referral program for your Fans, do so now. There is no better way to incent profitable behavior than to reward it.

A lot of organizations benefit from referrals or word-of-mouth but rely on "hope" that they come in. High-performing organizations make these referrals happen; they announce to their Fan base how the program works, reward appropriately those who generate revenue, and publicize the wins so that other Customer/Fans are motivated to participate.

## EXERCISE 5.1 AUDIENCE CHARACTERISTICS

1. Name two characteristics that help you identify your prospects and customers by need segment. Here you're looking for ways to figure out who is who in your database, sales lists, and personal interactions.

For example, maybe you identify a shopper by someone who downloads a whitepaper or you identify a looker as someone who opt-ins for a webinar.

A. Loiterer: _____     _____

B. Looker: _____     _____

C. Shopper: _____     _____

D. Buyer: _____     _____

E. Customer: _____     _____

F. Fan: _____     _____

# Chapter 6. The Messaging

## Audience Connections

Once we understand our audience by breaking it down into profiles and need segments, we need to be able to connect with them. Each need segment we defined –Loiterer, Looker, Shopper, Buyer, Customer, and Fan – needs to be addressed with a key message. Once we understand the key message, we can start to craft our marketing and positioning around that message.

The important thing to remember is that any one prospect will pass through many need segments before they become a Customer. And many Customers will develop into Fans. Each of these phases requires a different communication pattern.

Let's consider each need segment separately.

## Key Prospect Messages

The **Loiterer** is satisfied or misdirected. It's your responsibility to communicate clearly and effective two messages. First, what is your target market? And second, what do you do?

We can get to the heart of the matter by asking ourselves: with whom do we do our best work? This question is similar to asking what our target market is, but it's much more personal. It not only identifies a target client, but an ideal one.

What we do is generate results for our clients. We spent time in Chapter 3 discussing our One Big Result. Now, it's time to explain it.

We can fill in the phrases to create the key Loiterer message.

"We do our best work when we work with _____. The number one result they see is _____."

This one sentence brings together the target market and One Big Result in a way that is clear. The Loiterer will be able to tell if they're included in this brand promise or if it's meant for someone else. There should be no doubt to a prospect if they're in the target market.

We'll use these two examples throughout for continuity.

"We do our best work with affluent homeowners who have outgrown their existing homes but do not want to move. The number one result they see is improved quality of life while saving money."

"We do our best work with small business owners who need to grow but don't have a lot of capital. The number one result they see is a 34% increase in sales in 90 days."


The **Looker** has wants and preferences, but hasn't identified a need yet. They need to understand what your product means to them in a personal way.

The key message revolves around, "Why does it matter?" Often people act with their gut long before the brain gets involved. Therefore, our best first outreach is to connect emotionally.

Your product induces an emotional reaction when prospects see how their life is changed by what you do. This statement isn't overly dramatic. If you don't think your product changes people's lives, then you should find a new product. You need to be able to articulate how their lives will be changed, either in a before/after description or by simply stating how things will be in the future.

We fill in the phrase to create the key Looker message.

"After people become loyal customers, their lives change. Now, they experience _____."

This key message communicates two things. First, you want this prospect to become a loyal customer. That's not trivial; it's important to show faith in both the prospect and in your product that things will turn out well. Second, you communicate how the customer's life will change. This vision forms the basis of your Looker message.

Here are our examples.

"After people become loyal customers, their lives change. Now, they experience <u>a love of their home that they never had before. All while saving over $300,000.</u>"

"After people become loyal customer, their lives change. Now, they experience <u>no worry about money and more free time to spend with family and friends.</u>"

The **Shopper** has a need that needs fulfilling. That identified need forms the basis of the key Shopper message. We need to verbalize the need because sometimes our customer knows they have a need but can't put their finger on it; we need to name it in order to promise we can meet the need.

In each customer profile, there should be a single version of that need. If you can't pinpoint a single, primary need then you might have too many profiles mingled in one.

We fill in the phrase to create the key Shopper message.

"The number one need among our customers is _____; we meet that need by _____."

The key message here is to be able to show the Shopper that you understand their need and can fix their problem. You will need to do some connecting of the solution to the need. It may not be clear exactly how the two interact. But it's critical to show you know how to make the problem go away.

Here are our examples.

"The number one need among our customers is <u>more space in their home</u>; we meet that need by <u>delivering customer home renovation that meets their budget constraints</u>."

"The number one need among our customers is <u>more revenue and profit in their pockets</u>; we meet that need by <u>coaching business owners to re-position their products and targeting their efforts</u>."


The **Buyer** wants to buy – now. The need here is to figure out how to make the transaction happen as quickly as possible. All of the elements of the transaction need to be communicated: how, how much, where, what next?

Remember the example of the department store? You've had the experience of being frustrated by not being able to find the cashier or cash register, right? That's what happens to the Buyer when they can't transact their business. And oddly enough, many Buyers will leave quickly and frustrated if they can't fulfil their need.

Here, the customer profile may or may not matter. What matters is how you close the transaction. And you need to be able to explain it clearly.

We fill in the phrase to create the key Buyer message.

"In order to become a customer, a prospect needs to _____."

This is less about your Value Proposition and much more about your process. Of course, it does no good to communicate a poor process. You need to think carefully through the elements of the transaction itself. Reduce the number of steps to the bare minimum. Automate everything that can be automated.

Even if you're still working on your buying process, you need to be able to communicate the steps necessary to complete the transaction. This is particularly important for B2B services with invoicing or billing.

Often, companies like to "hold back" information about the process in order to force a conversation with a human being. There are times when this strategy can be useful, but be clear about the type of prospect you force into a one-on-one conversation versus one that can commit, opt-in, or transact through a self-service channel.

Here are our examples.

"In order to become a customer, a prospect needs to <u>sign off on a work order and make any down-payment</u>."

"In order to become a customer, a prospect needs to <u>sign a coaching agreement and make the first month's payment</u>."


## Key Customer Messages

Although we only have two major need segments for the audience that has purchased your product – Customer and Fan – there are a number of messages we need to be able to deliver in order to keep a Customer loyal.

We follow up the purchase with Information, Service, and Support. Once the **Customer** has had some interaction with our product or service, they may become dissatisfied. In order to detect that, we have to have a plan in place to measure customer satisfaction. Then, we need to deal with dissatisfied customers in a way that is consistent with our brand promise and the lifetime value of the Customer.

The Customer needs Information about the transaction – how to pay for the product, finance the product, obtain support, etc. This Information is part of the Customer experience. For online transactions, such Information is often the only tangible evidence, beyond the original receipt, that a transaction has taken place. It can be critical to Customer loyalty.

Support helps the customer use the product while Service helps the Customer in case of a problem. We fill in the phrase to create the key Customer message.

"In order to be most successful, our customers will need the following information: _____; service: _____; and support: _____."

Although you may not communicate it directly to the Customer, this represents your Customer Information, Service, and Support plan. Having one is the first step towards delivering on these promises. When done effectively, the customer will have a positive experience.

Here are our examples.

"In order to be most successful, our customers will need the following information: the schedule of work, the schedule of payments, and contact information for their superintendent; service: the phone numbers of all key team members along with the website address for submitting punch list items; support: continued monthly meetings with the planner in order to go over the schedule, any changes, and to ensure the quality expectations are met."

"In order to be most successful, our customers will need the following information: the signed coaching agreement, payment schedule, access to an online portal for information, and the coach contact information; service: the coach contact information in case of rescheduling issues or emergencies; support: the coach contact information and online portal to access materials assigned by the coach."

Another plan that needs to be articulated is the Customer satisfaction survey plan. We fill in the phrase:

"We check customer satisfaction by _____ every _____ (number/time frame)."

Here, one example will suffice.

"We check customer satisfaction by <u>surveying them</u> every <u>three months</u>."

If you find that there is a problem, you and your staff need to be empowered to deal with it. We fill in the phrase:

"When a problem occurs, _____ is/are empowered to fix it."

This plan ensures staff are chosen and directed to do whatever they can to fix the problem in a way that maintains the lifetime positive value for the Customer.

Note that since you are fixing problems in a way that maintains lifetime value, you will not "overpay" to fix a problem. You will do enough to make a Customer loyal again or to avoid other financial penalties, but you will not simply throw money at a Customer that is not a good fit for your business or will not remain loyal, anyway.

Again, one example will suffice.

"When a problem occurs, <u>all employees</u> are empowered to fix it."

Finally, the **Fan** is the ultimate asset of your business. Customers who actively participate in generating revenue for you are critical to your success. Fans need to be incented to refer new customers to your business. Don't expect that to happen by itself.

In addition to bringing brand new customers to the table, Fans are also a great source of repeat or up-sell business. You should have a plan in place to take advantage of those opportunities.

We fill in the following phrase to build our key Fan messaging.

"When a customer becomes a Fan, we offer _____ as an up/cross-sell and incent referrals by _____."

Here are our examples.

"When a customer becomes a Fan, we offer <u>upgrades or additional work</u> as an up/cross-sell and incent referrals by <u>offering a 5% referral bonus</u>."

"When a customer becomes a Fan, we offer <u>an upgraded program at a discount</u> as an up/cross-sell and incent referrals by <u>offering a free session when a new referral signs up</u>."

## Audience Channels

Once we've established what we want to say to our audience, we need to discuss how we're going to say it. That means selecting the appropriate channel for each customer profile and need segment.

There is not one answer for everyone. You need to know your customer profiles well. Where do they "hang out?" Are they comfortable doing business online or would they rather deal with a human being? In any case, you need to select one or two preferred channels in order to deliver the messages you've crafted.

Let's review several of your options and talk about their pros and cons.

### *Website*

Your business should have a website. (If it doesn't, stop right now and create one.) It doesn't need to be fancy, but it does need to communicate.

Websites should not just be online brochures, but they do not need to be interactive with all the bells and whistles, either. This depends on your target market. But generally, some of the messages you want to distribute will be communicated via your website.

Your Loiterer and Looker will want to see your website so the messages you chose for them will need to be present here.

The Shopper and Buyer may want to see your website, assuming you can assist the prospect in selecting and purchasing your product online. If not, then some of this may best be handled in person.

A website is a great place to provide Customer information. In addition, automated referral programs can be a quick way to monetize your existing Fans.

## E-mail

Although similar to website content, e-mail is different in that it can be highly personalized. We're seeing that same trend in websites, as well, but it's much easier and more common to see it done with e-mail.

E-mail is a great channel to connect with people who have already built some level of trust with you in that they have agreed to communicate via e-mail. E-mail is not for Loiterers.

Automated e-mail communication, often called an autoresponder, is perfect for Lookers and Shoppers. Because e-mail is great for storytelling and selling, a well-crafted autoresponder helps Lookers become Shoppers and Shoppers become Buyers.

E-mail should migrate Buyers over to a shopping cart or salesperson to close the transaction.

But e-mail can also be a useful tool to communicate with Customers and Fans about upcoming sales, especially when personalized to their interests. Also, a Customer newsletter that continues to educate and allows the Customer to further monetize their investment in your product will produce Fans faster than almost any other technique.

I shouldn't have to mention this, but I feel like I should: There is a difference between permission-based outbound e-mail and spam. I am not in favor of spam in any form. Often, we think of spam as the completely unsolicited mass e-mails that come from companies we don't even have a relationship with. That is obvious. But spam is also taking a business card and adding it to your mailing list without the permission of the person. Receiving a business card from someone does not give you permission to mass e-mail them commercial offers. Many companies still do this. It is spam; it is not only ineffective, it's just wrong.

It's perfectly okay to e-mail people personally with an individually crafted e-mail but don't just add them to a list and "blast" them with the latest newsletter.

## Outbound Call Center

Outbound calling, or telemarketing, often has a bad name, and for good reason. This very appropriate and useful tool is often misused by companies, which makes it difficult for everyone.

Generally speaking, if you sell to consumers, outbound calling to prospects that do not already have a relationship with your business requires a great deal of compliance. You need to get Do Not Call lists (at least in the United States) and manage opt-outs, etc. In some countries, the practice is forbidden by law. I don't recommend it for most of my clients. The uplift is small, the effort large, and the "black-eye" effect can be even larger.

Thus, do not outbound call Loiterers if you are a B2C company.

For businesses, this can be a bit different. The regulatory piece doesn't (yet) apply as heavily, and most companies are left to police themselves. Thus, I recommend a gentle hand, and a small and select list. The idea is to make a carefully placed and well-researched phone call to a key decision maker. Done right, this can be very effective.

However, once a prospect has entered your sales cycle, outbound calling at the appropriate time with the appropriate offer can be useful.

Make sure you know your clear call-to-action and be reasonably sure that the call will be welcomed.

How do you know that? From the data.

All throughout your sales cycle, you will be collecting data from your prospects to know into which need segment they fall. When they provide you with data that indicates their need segment has changed – by interacting with you on your website, downloading a piece of collateral information, or by talking with a sales representative – you can reach out with a pre-planned, specific campaign.

Generally speaking, however, this is usually only welcomed when customers are ready to engage in a conversation about their needs and how they relate to your offering. Thus, outbound calling can be appropriate for Shoppers and Buyers. I typically discourage it for Lookers.

## Inbound Call Center

Inbound calling is completely different than outbound calling. It's a great idea to encourage prospects to engage with a human being, assuming it makes sense from a cost perspective.

Inbound calling is best used for Lookers, Shoppers, and Buyers with the return on investment increasing the further up the ladder you go. I recommend it when the numbers support it. To know this, you will need to run a simulation of your marketing campaign and know the return on investment for each customer profile.

A general point, however, is that you want to make access to the sales process as easy as possible. For your inbound sales numbers, drop the interactive voice response and multi-level menus. Don't even ask them to "Press one for sales and two for service." Have a separate number. Get your inbound callers to a person as quickly as possible.

Larger organizations should not split sales staff across customer profiles that could reasonably call the same number. In other words: stop transferring people! Train your people to handle the sales conversation. Give them a script, if necessary. Move to the next step without needing to transfer.

## Print Collateral

Conversion from print collateral, alone, not associated with a direct marketing campaign is typically so weak that I don't consider it a viable strategy. Direct mail can be effective. So can handing out a brochure during a pre-planned sales call. However, leaving brochures for people to pick up at the laundromat or dropping off fliers at another office to be displayed are poor uses of resources.

The problem with most print collateral is that the writer and designer don't know the audience who will read it. That's especially true if it's meant to be generic or left at a laundromat.

Print collateral should target one need segment, and generally not Loiterers. It should include language consistent with the need segment and provide a call-to-action that is aligned with the chosen campaign.

In other words, don't design a brochure with pictures, case studies, but no facts, and end with a "Buy Now" call-to-action. That means you've been talking to Lookers, but treating them like Buyers. That kind of mismatch is all too common.

In direct marketing, it's much easier. You have a list of prospects which you (hopefully) have segmented by need segment. They get the collateral material that suits their need. And a call-to-action that is consistent with where they are in the sales process.

## *Live People*

Believe it or not, in this electronic world, there is still room for human beings in the sales process.

Human beings are the most flexible and most expensive sales resource we have. Face-to-face meetings can be incredibly effective yet very expensive. Sometimes, there is no other substitute.

I have personally flown halfway around the world for a single sales meeting because no other sales process could be used. Just be wise about it.

The trick with using people is that they need to be trained to stay on message. Without the right training, sales representatives have a difficult time assessing the need segment of the person they're talking to. In addition, they don't know when the prospect has changed need segments, and thus their messaging needs to change.

Assuming it's economical to use a human being in a portion of the sales process (and it's isn't always so), it's important they understand what role they play and how best to stay in line with the marketing campaign as a whole.

I discuss this in greater detail in Section 5.

For each need segment and customer profile, you should be able to find two different channels that will fit. In the exercises that follow, you will write out the messaging and channel delivery. Together, the connection and the channel become your communication plan.

## EXERCISE 6.1 KEY PROSPECT MESSAGES

**Create your key prospect messages by filling in the blanks.**

1. For the Loiterer:

We do our best work when we work with _____
The number one result they see is _____
_____.

2. For the Looker:

After people become loyal customers, their lives change. Now, they
experience _____
_____.

3. For the Shopper:

The number one need among our customers is _____;
we meet that need by delivering _____.

4. For the Buyer:

In order to become a customer, a prospect needs to _____
_____.

## EXERCISE 6.2 KEY CUSTOMER MESSAGES

**Develop your key customer messages. Fill in the blanks below.**

1. For the new customer:

In order to be most successful, our customer will need the following information: _____,
service: _____,
and support: _____.

2. For customer satisfaction:

We check customer satisfaction by _____
every _____ _____ (number/time frame)

3. For dissatisfied customers:

When a problem occurs, _____ is/are empowered to fix it.

4. For fans:

When a customer becomes a "fan", we offer _____
as an up/cross-sell and incent referrals by _____.

## EXERCISE 6.3 COMMUNICATION PLAN

Identify two channels or methods by which you can deliver the messages you just created for each customer profile you created. Note: many may be the same across profiles, so you can indicate for which profiles the channels may be different.

1. For the Loiterer:

1. _____

2. _____

2. For the Looker:

1. _____

2. _____

3. For the Shopper:

1. _____

2. _____

4. For the Buyer:

1. _____

2. _____

5. For the new Customer:

1. _____

2. _____

6. To deliver Customer satisfaction surveys:

1. _____

2. _____


7. For the dissatisfied Customer:

1. _____

2. _____


8. For the Fan:

1. _____

2. _____

# Section 3. The Business Model

# Chapter 7. Monetization

## The Goal: New Stable and Recurring Revenue

It's the one question that strikes dread in the heart of every entrepreneur: How are you going to monetize that?

It's true that ideas are more powerful than the Business Models that support them, but you still have to have a Business Model. And if you're like most successful service professionals, you only have one: hourly billing.

Hourly billing is a great model. Especially to start. It lowers the risk for the client: they only pay for what they get. And it lowers the risk for the service delivery professional: they get paid for what they do.

The challenge is that there are also downsides to that model. First off, what happens if you're not working? Of course, you don't get paid, but you also don't have any cushion in case you have a dry spell. You could save and price appropriately (see Chapter 9 on appropriate pricing.) Many business owners, however, just don't know enough about their own work to "gross up," as they say, for the downtime.

Many books on consulting will tell you to abandon the hourly rate model and move to the fixed price model. This, they claim, will let you escape the trap of low earnings and get rich quickly.

It's true that fixed pricing can be lucrative, but it also has a dark downside. If you are not good at scoping out work, you can get burned. You could be working long past the hourly equivalent of that job — essentially working for free.

The fixed price model also puts you in the unenviable position of having to "manage scope." That's the nice way of saying "no" to all those things your client wants you to do for free under your "fixed price."

So why do the books keep telling you that that's your answer? Mostly because the vast majority of entrepreneurs will never get past the point at which they can't charge any more for their work. The argument goes that if you identify the value in what you do, you can charge a multiple of that value.

That may be true up to a certain point. But every offer you make doesn't get made in a vacuum. There are alternatives for the client: doing it themselves or not doing anything at all. Once your fixed price is so high that the "do it yourself" option becomes cheaper, then you've lost your ability to offer your services at a high price. So when fixed prices cap out, you're stuck with the same problem. A little better off than before, but stuck just the same.

Monetization means not concentrating all your product or service in one place.

Another challenge many small business people face is having one customer represent a significant portion of their income. If that customer doesn't pay or, worse, leaves, the business is left high and dry.

If you have any customer that represents more than 10% of your income, you're concentrated too heavily in one place. Of course, your Business Model may have created that problem, but we're trying to fix that by creating more diverse income streams. So what's the answer?

The goal of scalable monetization should be to create New and Diverse income that is Stable and Recurring.

New, meaning from sources you don't have today.

Diverse, meaning earning no more than 10% from any one customer.

Stable, meaning immune from seasonal and non-seasonal starts and stops.

Recurring, meaning you can count on cash coming in on a regular basis.

We'll address each one individually.

## Creating New Revenue

In the search for new income, we actually have to look for new opportunities. In some cases, this means new ideas: opportunities to make money in ways that we didn't think about before. The best way to think about this is to think about your existing customers and how you would make new money from them. This is a little bit different than simply finding new customers. Simply finding new customers is growing your existing product. What we want to do is to find new products.

As a mental exercise, think about your existing customers. As we know, it's easiest to generate new revenue from an existing customer than to find a new customer. If you had to go back to your existing customer and find another way to make money, what could you possibly offer that would be of interest to them? What other areas can you generate income from? Think about the service that you actually provide. Usually, your service occupies a small piece of your customer's business life span.

For example, maybe you provide human resource training, such as diversity and teamwork, and the customer calls you when there's a training need. There are clearly tasks that happen before they need you and tasks that happen after they need you. Are there any ways that you can provide services in those additional areas? Can you provide consulting that helps your customer understand that they need the training, or can you provide support after the training has occurred? Considering the scope of the services you offer and expanding that scope to include things that occur either before or after the services that you currently provide is one very good way of finding new revenue from existing customers.

Another way to think about generating new revenue is to think about delivering the exact same service that you provide today but in a different format. For example, can you offer your consulting service in the form of training? What if you record your materials and provide it in a different format? What if you move from dealing with individuals to talking to groups? Can you do peer facilitation instead of one-on-one work, or is there another way to format your materials so that it could be used in a different way?

Can you take something that you do "live" and move it to the internet? Can you take something that you do on the internet and just use the audio? Can you take audio and add video to it? Can you take video and turn it into a "live" event? Can you take a presentation that you would normally deliver in a conference boardroom and deliver it in a conference room in a "live" session? Thinking about a different medium for your existing content is another way to extract new revenue from an existing client.

## Creating Diverse Revenue

Another important monetization strategy in your Business Model is to make sure that your revenue comes from diverse sources. One of the challenges of small businesses is that they tend to concentrate revenue with a few clients. This is particularly true with consulting companies or single-operator service businesses. That happens naturally because people who are in the service industry will work with the same client over and over again, and often that client will become their best client or their most prominent client. When you spend so much time servicing your primary client and don't have time to market and sell to new customers, you will find your revenue dominated by one or two particular customers.

This is a particularly dangerous thing to occur in your business at any stage, but as you start to scale it can be absolutely deadly. As you start to become bigger, you might find that your service offering changes and that you have to give up some of the clients that you have today in order to move to a different service model. If any one of those clients were to not fit the new model and you have to give up that revenue, it could be a devastating change to your income.

We measure diversity of income by looking at what percentage of your top line revenue comes from any one client. If you have any one client that represents more than about 10% of your total revenue for the year, you should consider that client as overly contributing to your business. This is dangerous because if the client were to stop paying or suddenly cancel their service with you, it would represent a huge drop in income, which you would have to find a way to make up. As you look to scale and grow your business, you don't want to be fighting income losses from large customers who leave.

Unfortunately, there are only two ways to resolve diversity of income. The first, which is not very pleasant, is to get rid of the client that is contributing a lot of revenue to your business. Most companies don't want to and can't do this; in fact, that is usually not the right thing to do. But you should think very carefully about whether or not this client fits the model and the concept of the business you're trying to develop so that when it does become palatable and reasonable for you to move away from that particular client, you can do so.

The second answer is to simply increase your revenue, but not from that that same client. This seems obvious, but it turns out to be difficult to do in practice only because most business owners with a very large client are used to going back to that client repeatedly when they need revenue. It takes a mindset shift to pursue revenue in other places.

If you happen to have a client who's generating more than 10% of your current revenue, there isn't anything necessarily wrong with that today, but it's definitely something to pay attention to as you grow so that this situation doesn't continue. It's also something to consider when you think about creating a new product or a new concept for the business you're planning on scaling. You definitely don't want to create a situation in which you could create this problem again or make the one you have today worse.

Your best bet is to find a diverse product that you can scale across a number of different customers so that your revenue is derived from multiple sources. This protects you in case of any one of your clients doesn't pay, cancels their service or, worse, goes out of business. You need to create stable income. This is a critical factor in the stability of most companies and, in fact, when accountants look at income statements, they worry about companies that have their revenue concentrated with one particular customer. This is definitely something you want to avoid by creating a product that can sell across different companies.

## Creating Recurring Revenue

One of the hallmarks of a healthy company is the presence of recurring income. Your goal as a business owner should be to create recurring income so that you can get rid of cash flow ups and downs that typically come with service-oriented businesses that have grown to the point at which they need to expand. Imagine a business with recurring income: there would be fewer windfall months and fewer lean months. Every month of your revenue should be steady and stable. This means flattening out your cash flow. The best way to flatten out your cash flow is to accelerate it and create back-end value.

The way to think about whether or not you can create recurring revenue with your existing product is to think about your current pricing model. Do you typically charge a big, upfront fee to start a project? Is there a way that you can continue to add value for your existing customer in order to generate recurring revenue from them? In your current pricing model, how much of your revenue is variable?

In other words, does it change from month to month based on whether or not your customer actually uses the service that you provide? Is there a way for you to flatten out that revenue so that you can collect the same amount every month, even if on some months you do slightly more work than during other months so that you can have predictable revenue every month? If you can't flatten out your existing service revenue, maybe there are other services that you can add in to fill in the low periods in order to flatten out the revenue from your customers.

We'll talk a little bit more about pricing in a later chapter, but it's important to think about what average monthly revenue for your customer might mean to your business if you have highs and lows. This means doing a little bit of analysis of what your revenue looks like over the past twelve months to determine your "average" monthly revenue.

You're also looking for other patterns such as increases in revenue. You might find that the average amount you're charging a particular customer is actually going up over time. If that's the case, you don't want to look backwards over the last twelve months, but look at the percent increase in revenue over the last few months and see if you can project it into the future if you think that dynamic will continue.

In some sense, pricing services with a retainer is a bit of an art form and requires some discussion and negotiation with each client, but making the decision to change to a retainer-based model instead of an hourly model is more of a challenge to the mindset of the business owner. Once that change is made and communicated confidently to each of your clients, most will eventually get on board and participate in the new program. You may have clients that refuse to participate in a retainer program; you can decide if you want to make an exception for those clients or if that would create a problem for you. You might decide to move on and help that client transition to another service provider. You should not in any way continue billing on an hourly basis as you start to scale and grow.

Another way to create recurring revenue is to turn your service into a product. Products can be sold on a subscription basis. Once something is automated and turned into a process, most clients feel comfortable subscribing as long as they feel like they're getting value on an ongoing basis and have an opportunity to get out of the contract should that value stop recurring. You have to think carefully about services that may not have an ongoing value. If you do set-up services or get people started on a process that becomes very difficult to productize by itself, you will need to think about ways to create ongoing value in order justify ongoing fees.

## Creating Stable Revenue

One of the final challenges that business owners face in trying to monetize a scalable product is getting rid of their seasonal highs and low periods. Creating steady income throughout the year is important for your business. You do not want to grow a business that has seasonal low points. As your business grows, it will require greater expenses to run, including potentially hiring more people. When that happens, those low points, which are mildly annoying at present, will start to become deadly. It will be important in your business to remove those seasonal highs and lows from your Business Model. Generally speaking, this requires you to think about another service for your target market, or a different service or product that you can sell during those low periods.

Here are some things to ask yourself to help you understand how to construct a stable revenue model. Think about your current target market during your down time: what can you deliver that's of value during that period. Don't think about your current services; focus on additional services. What other assets and materials do you have just lying around that could be used during your down time. Don't think about your current market, but focus on what you could use your inventory or tools or personnel to build during that down time. Then, when your current target market is laying low, who is actually busy and doing something?

Again, don't think about what you could deliver to them; think simply about who is active during that time. Filling in low points with high points from other areas or markets is a diversification tactic we call "hedging." Investors use this technique to cover downturns in the market. You can use this same approach with your business by diversifying the portfolio of products and services you offer, as well as the target markets to which you offer them. This will provides you with the opportunity to fill in the gaps and flatten out your income so that you're getting a stable revenue string throughout the year.

## EXERCISE 7.1 CREATING NEW AND DIVERSE REVENUE WHICH IS STABLE AND RECURRING.

New revenue

1. If you could no longer get a new customer, and all growth had to be from existing or former customers, what would you sell them? _____

_____

2. In which other areas can you generate revenue from your existing customer base? _____

_____

3. In which other formats can you re-purpose existing product or materials and sell them? _____

_____


Diverse revenue

1. Which of your customers represent more than 10% of your current total revenue? (Note: if you have fewer than 10 customers, then one of them definitely does.)

_____

_____

2. Thinking of those customers who represent a high percentage of your revenue, will they continue to be customers as you grow and develop your new concept? If not, how will you replace that income?

_____

_____

3. How much more money would you have to make so that none of your current customers represent more than 10% of your total revenue?

_____

_____

_____

Stable revenue

1. What does your current target market need during your "low period?" _____

_____

2. What assets or materials do you have during your "low period" that you can use? _____

_____

3. When your current target market is laying low, who is busy and needs something? _____

_____

Recurring revenue

1. How can you move from hourly pricing to retainer pricing? What will your new retainer amount be? _____

_____

2. What value can you create after the first engagement in order to continue billing for services after the first portion is complete?

_____

_____

3. What product can you create from your service that you simply charge for on a recurring basis? _____

_____

# Chapter 8. Creating and Refining Your Product

## Get Ready for Imperfection

The first thing we need to explore when we talk about your offering is finding the Minimum Viable Solution. This is very similar to the concept of a Minimum Viable Product, but since we're talking about product offerings that may involve services, I prefer to use the term Solution.

A Minimum Viable Solution has a couple of important elements. It is Minimal and it is Viable, but the one thing it is *not* is perfect. In my experience, the biggest challenge in getting people to create a Minimum Viable Solution is accepting the fact that it will not be perfect. It will not be the perfect thing that you have been thinking your market absolutely needs, but it will be an important step toward getting out into the market.

This is a psychological barrier that a lot of people have difficulty overcoming, and if we can't get past the idea that we need to be able to fail in the marketplace in order to eventually succeed, we'll never get a solution to the market. It's often the case that people allow the perfect to become the enemy of the good. It doesn't mean we put out garbage because there is an element of being Viable, but it's important to know that a Minimum Viable Solution may not be what we think is important or is good for the market in the end, but right now we're just trying to get a product out. We will put our "baby", our product, our solution, out into the marketplace, with all of its warts and problems, in order to gain feedback. We need to be open to that feedback and not overly sensitive to it. Every time we hear a "No," we need to listen and view it as an opportunity to find out what went wrong. Every single time somebody rejects our offer, we should try to hear the reasons so we can put something better next time. If we don't listen, we will simply be thrashing around without knowing where we're going or what the market's looking for.

The smart thing to do is test the waters. That means creating something that isn't the perfect product, it isn't the perfect solution, but that's okay; we have to be okay with imperfection and failure during the short term in order to generate a Minimum Viable Solution.

Most often, when people have difficulty selling their product or solution, it's because the product they created doesn't really fit the need so they have to start over again. Starting over requires thinking through, from the beginning, exactly what's needed in the marketplace. We need to learn about what people actually are going to buy. If we spend all of our time creating the perfect solution, the perfect product, we'll discover that we spent a lot of time chasing a direction in which no one's going to spend money.

People are scared of failure because they think failure is the end. Failure is not the end, but it can become the end if we're not prepared for it. What we need to do is put a feedback mechanism in place that will allow us to learn from the failure and improve, and put out something better next time. As we go through this section, we're going to learn what it means to generate a Minimum Viable Solution and how to put a feedback mechanism in place so we can learn from it. Without that feedback mechanism, it is possible to fail but never learn from that failure.

In this process, it's important to listen to the market, have some way of collecting information from the marketplace and feed it back into our product or solution development cycle. Without that, we can make very serious errors in judgment.

The other thing to remember is that whatever we put out today may not be the right product in the future. Even if we have the perfect solution, we would still need a feedback mechanism along with an understanding that, in the future, we might fail. We need to understand what that failure might look like and how to recognize it when it happens so we can adjust our product, adjust our solution, adjust to the market, and come out with something better next time.

All of these things will bring us to a market-leading solution, because a market-leading solution is one that listens to the market, fulfills its need, delivers on its One Big Result, and does so in a cost-effective way so it can be offered at a lowest possible price. This generates a profit that's consistent with the value you're generating. All of these things are critical for you to be able to deliver your One Big Result.

Before we get started on understanding what's behind a Minimum Viable Solution, you need to be accept that your first solution will not be perfect and may, in fact, fail but that is a constructive part of the process.

## Get Minimal

The first step behind creating the Minimum Viable Solution is to get minimal. Remember, it's important to internalize that we need to be ready to have an imperfect solution go out in the market. That requires us to emotionally disconnect from our solution because we think we know what the market needs.

What does it mean to get minimal? It means we are going to have to get rid of all of the nice-to-haves and move to just what is required to deliver our One Big Result.

The best way to do this exercise is to take a piece of paper. At the top of the page, write down the One Big Result that you promised your market you'll deliver. You are looking at relaunching a product, or already have an existing product in mind. If you don't have an existing product, think about the product you would like to launch. What we need to do now is diagram the process.

Start on the left side of the page and write down all of the inputs to your current process or your desired process, every step along the way all the way, to the outputs of the process, which will go on the right side of the page. Keep the inputs separate from the outputs.

This is very much like a flowchart; there are things that run in parallel and may come in from the top or the bottom. In those cases, we want to make sure that they feed into the process at the appropriate location, where the output of the process requires it in order to perform the next step.

Essentially, you'll be creating a workflow diagram of how your product works. All of the things that can be done in parallel should be listed in separate rows. Think carefully about each box on that flowchart because each should represent a step, either to be taken by the user, the product, or system in your solution.

Once you've got everything down on paper, it's time for the hard part – to start taking things away one at a time. We're going to keep track of everything that we remove by recording them in a list in the order that they're removed. It's important to we keep a list of what we remove in the order in which we delete them since later in the process we may start putting some of these features back and we want to put them back in the reverse order that we removed them. It's not unlike dismantling a mechanical device: you put the pieces you remove on the ground in the order in which you removed them so that you can reassemble the mechanism in the correct order.

To do this, we must ask ourselves: "What is the least important piece of this product or process?" On the piece of paper, note the least important element. This may be very difficult; you may think that everything is absolutely necessary, but look at those items that are on the parallel path. Are they required? Are they 'extras?' Think about your One Big Result and what is required to actually deliver that One Big Result.

Make sure that at each stage, if you remove a step, you're not removing something will cause the process to break downstream. For example, if the output requires a step in the front, then you can't remove that step without removing the output of that step. Just remove one block at a time. You'll know you're done when you're left with a single path from input to output in which every step is required and there are no extras.

This generally means that the parallel paths that are feeding into the process are gone. Think about the minimum inputs necessary and the minimum outputs necessary to deliver your One Big Result. If you're having a difficult time doing this, start on the output side. Delete output items that are not required to deliver your One Big Result. Start deleting what's least important and write it down as you delete it from the process map. As you start to delete items from the right (the output) side of the process, you'll find that there are items to the left (the input side) that were required to generate the outputs that no longer exist and are no longer necessary.

If you think you're done but don't have a single path, think long and hard again about whether or not every piece of that diagram is required, because you need to get down to a minimum part of your Minimum Viable Solution.

When you're finished, the number of inputs will be the minimum required to achieve the output you want, and the number of outputs you're left with represent the deliverable of your Minimum Viable Solution.

Remember, you must disconnect emotionally so that you can take things away until you're left with the bare essentials. It's important that you go through this process even if you think that your current product is as minimal as it can be because often when a product is not selling, it's because we need a lower barrier to entry to acquire customers. Often, a lower barrier to entry product is simply a lesser-functioning, less expensive, version of your existing product.

We'll get to that in another section but this will help us understand exactly what is required to deliver on the One Big Result. Later on, we may find that an even smaller result is necessary as a first step, and so this is a good exercise. It's important to note that what you're left with is not a viable solution – only a minimal one. You should have a list of steps in ascending order of importance because in the next stage we will start putting some of those pieces back in, one at a time, as we get feedback from the marketplace.

## Get Viable

The next step in creating your Minimum Viable Solution is taking your minimum solution and making it viable. In order to do this, you'll need to get out of the office and into the marketplace, itself. The biggest mistake that most people make in creating the viable part of a Minimum Viable Product is forgetting the core question: "Will people pay for it?" There's a lot of advice out there about creating fake landing pages or creating surveys to ask people if they would buy certain products and how much they would pay for them, but such surveys tend to be unreliable, while landing pages that simply ask people to opt in in order to determine their willingness to buy something generally don't give you a good sense of whether they would actually pay for it. You have to get people to give you money in order to know whether or not you have something viable. We're going to start with the minimum part of our solution that we created in the last stage and see if we can sell it.

You may say, "This is difficult because I may have pieces I can build, or I may have to go through a development effort." At this stage, we don't know if what we have is something that we're going to do full time. We don't know if it's viable, so we don't want to spend a lot of unnecessary time developing it. The trick here is focusing on delivery, not scalability. That requires us to be a bit creative and think about how we might deliver on each of these stages of the process in such a way that we can perform it inexpensively.

Here are three questions that you should ask yourself about every step of the process: 1. Can you perform the process manually? 2. Can you perform the process after they pay? 3. Can you teach your customer how to perform the process? In each case, the question focuses on the outcome of having a paid customer rather the scalability of the process.

You need to get creative to get viable. In Dan Norris' book, *The Seven-Day Startup, You Don't Learn Until You Launch*, he describes several examples of how people have tested their Minimum Viable Product in unique ways. In one case, an entrepreneur interested in launching a daily deals site for wine tested the hypothesis through a party. (Don't worry about making it scalable; worry about seeing if people will actually pay you.)

One last note on surveys: research consistently shows that people often overstate in surveys whether they'll pay and how much they'll pay. When it comes down to actually taking the credit card out of their wallet and processing a charge, people often change their minds at the last minute. Don't rely on surveys without expert statistical help to interpret the answers.

Each step of testing the viability of the product should give you information about whether you have something that is scalable. Get feedback from your customers, especially the ones that do not give you money; from those who do give you money, it's important to know what part of the process failed for them and whether they got the promised One Big Result. If you choose to add things back into the process, look at the list that you created when you removed them and add back what you removed in reverse order; these are the things that you thought were fairly important to the process.

This will require a series of tests as you add additional features back into your Minimum Viable Solution in order for you to get something viable. Because you'll be testing multiple options in a short period of time, it will be important for you to focus on quick delivery and not scalability. Don't worry about being able to deliver this solution to hundreds or thousands or tens of thousands of customers. You only need to test a few customers to see if they will pay. If they will, you can go ahead and make it scalable after the fact.

This is very difficult for some companies to do, especially software companies that have lots of software developers ready to start coding. My advice is very similar to Guy Kawasaki's advice for startup software companies: first, consult; then build tools to make the consulting easier; and finally sell the tools. Apply that same thought process to whatever product or solution you're developing. This often requires you to deliver something in a very manual, labor-intensive manner for your first several customers. Remember: we're not trying to scale at this stage; we're trying to see whether or not someone will pay you for what you created.

Companies are often surprised to learn how little functionality they need to deliver in order to create a product that generates revenues. It may not be the same amount of money that you're hoping to generate from a final product, but since you are relaunching, we may start off with a smaller version of the product in order to generate a customer list that you can turn to later and deliver up-sale value. We'll talk about that process in a later section.

Right now, we want to make sure that a Minimum Viable Solution is selling and generating revenue for the company.

## Launch Now. No, Really; Now.

Once you've figured out a way to deliver your minimum product in order to test viability, the next step is to get it out into the marketplace as quickly as possible. Conventional wisdom is that you never have a second chance to make a first impression, and while that may be true on an individual basis, it rarely holds true for entire marketplaces. At this stage we're simply testing the viability of your product with a few potential customers. Hopefully you've generated enough interest from those customers to be able to continue to sell or up-sell as you improve the process.

Many entrepreneurs get stuck on this step and delay their launch until the product is perfect. (Think about it: Microsoft never delivers a perfect product; its first release is always full of bugs). We have to get comfortable with the fact that we'll fail, and might potentially fail several times before we understand what is viable in the marketplace. There is no such thing as a perfect product; if we wait until we have one, we will never get into the marketplace. You don't have a product-oriented company until you have a product launch. I don't care how many strategy meetings or how many off-sites you have: you need to get your solution out in the marketplace.

One more note on getting feedback from customers: ask users what they like, what they don't like, what they want, and what they don't want. Don't try to be Steve Jobs and fall into the trap of saying that users don't know what they want. That's bogus. Users know what they want. As soon as you become famous and have a lot of money and capital backing, you can be Steve Jobs, but that will have to come later, after this company is a success. Unless you earn that reputation, backing and money, just get out there and find out what people want and deliver that One Big Result to meet their needs. You don't know better than the user who just paid you.

During the test process, if you have to add things back in order to make a solution viable or customers happy, react only to the feedback that paying customers give you. Don't listen to the community that didn't bother to buy your product since you don't know if reacting to that feedback will actually generate a sale. Your Minimum Viable Solution is built step by step by adding pieces back into your minimum solution based on *paid* user feedback.

One of the biggest mistakes that companies make is by not having a feedback loop in place. That means every single customer needs to be surveyed and talked to on a regular basis. This is at the beginning when we're not trying to be scalable; don't try to automate this portion of the process. The founder of the company, himself, should call the customers and ask them how they're using the product, what they'd like to see more of, and whether or not they're got your promised One Big Result. Don't trust this to automated surveys or autoresponders. Collect feedback on a person–to-person basis. Make a phone call. Send an e-mail. Have an in-person conversation, if necessary, but get the feedback and make the changes.

Set a goal to do this as quickly as possible. Set that goal now. Don't wait until you've read the rest of the book. This is enough for you to be able to make a decision about how quickly you're going to be able to get a product out into the marketplace. Every single day you wait you lose potential revenues and potential feedback from paying customers.

In the vast majority of cases, companies sit on a potential product that they can launch within ninety days. Make it a goal to create a Minimum Viable Solution and launch it. Just get something out there. It will be minimum and it will just be step one, but you'll never know what will become of the product until you get user feedback.

**EXERCISE 8.1 GET MINIMAL**

One Big Result: _____

Diagram your solution process in a workflow diagram. On the left include all inputs to the process. On the right include all outputs to the process. Connect processes together in order with arrows connecting steps that are required for the following step.

Start removing steps from the process that are not required to deliver your One Big Result. Keep a list of the steps you remove *in order of importance*. Start removing the least important steps until you are left with a single process flow from left to right where everything is required and nothing is extraneous.

Removed Steps:

1. _____

2. _____

3. _____

4. _____

Etc.

## EXERCISE 8.2 GET VIABLE

Look at your minimum solution workflow. List each step and how you will deliver that process - either with an existing process or manually so you can launch. Your goal is to deliver something to the marketplace in 90 days or less.

Step 1. _____

    Delivery method: _____


Step 2. _____

    Delivery method: _____


Step 3. _____

    Delivery method: _____


Step 4. _____

    Delivery method: _____


Step 5. _____

    Delivery method: _____


Step 6. _____

    Delivery method: _____

Etc.

# Chapter 9. Appropriate Pricing

## Scalable Pricing Models

There are a number of different pricing models available for your business. But not all of them are scalable. In Chapter 7 on Monetization, we discussed the need for stable and recurring revenue. The pricing models we discuss here will reflect that need.

Recurring revenue means finding a pricing model that is repeatable. One-time fees generally create an irregular pattern of cash flow and make it more difficult to manage your company's finances. Many business owners like one-time fees because it accelerates getting cash into the business. That's definitely a plus, but if it does so at a long-term risk to the business, it becomes a disadvantage rather than an advantage.

Products and services pricing is based upon three major components: cost of goods sold, operating expenses, and profit margin.

If you sell something that requires you to purchase goods or services first, that cost is the cost of goods sold. If you manufacture a product, the raw materials cost you money and thus represent cost of goods sold. If you provide a service and outsource some of it, that outsourcing cost is also the cost of goods sold. You have to price to recoup your cost of goods sold, and you should do so in a way that, as much as possible, matches your cash outlay.

Many business owners will price their product or service using recurring revenue and then finance the cost of goods sold over a period of time. Unless your business is a finance company, this is a bad idea.

Understanding the ins and outs of finance, the risk of your customer not paying or canceling their payment plan before you recoup your investment, and the implicit cost of financing are probably not your strong suit.

These kinds of calculations are the responsibilities of banks. And in 2008 we saw what happens when they got it wrong. Don't be in the business of financing your customers where you have to make a cash outlay. Cover those costs as quickly as possible, preferably in advance.

You will also have operating expenses. Operating expenses are the costs you incur to run your business but that aren't directly attributable to an individual customer. For example, if you provide website design and implementation services. You may have people responsible for project management. You may also outsource website design. While the price you pay to the website designer for a customer is a cost of goods sold, the cost of labor for internal project management is an operating expense.

Sometimes there isn't a clear line between the two. Check with your accountant for further guidance, but generally speaking, the operating expenses recur while the cost of goods sold is related specifically to the product or service you sell.

When you price your product or service, you must recoup your operating expenses. Since these are recurring expenses, you need to know how many products you sell, and how to divide the ongoing expenses by that number of products. If you sell different products, you can allocate the expenses across the products according to their different prices.

For example, if you sell two products – a $900 product and a $100 product – and you typically sell five of the $900 product per month while you sell twenty of the $100 product per month, then your total revenue is $4500 of your higher-priced product and $2000 of your lower-priced product. Since your total revenue is $6500, your expenses should be allocated at 70% to the higher-priced product ($4500 divided by 6500 units) and the remaining 30% to the lower-priced product.

Obviously, this is more challenging when you have lots of products, but the calculation doesn't have to be exact.

Since operating expenses are recurring, so should your revenue. Find a way to provide ongoing value to your customer to justify the cost. If you have to outsource some of that work in order to provide that value, remember that that additional cost is a cost of goods sold and should be factored into the price.

The final component of pricing is profit. This component is the hardest for business owners to determine. At its simplest, profit is whatever you decide it should be. But there are good and bad ways to set your profit margin.

Pricing should be set to achieve a reasonable level of profitability, take into consideration availability of your resources, and balance the market need. We'll cover each of these three concepts separately.

## Pricing for Profitability

How much is the right amount of profit? This is the million-dollar question. There is no easy answer.

Pricing experts will tell you that the right answer is "whatever the market will bear." And while that's true, how do you know how much the market will bear? In short, there's no way to know for sure until you start to test pricing.

When companies are small, they charge whatever they can. If a customer balks, the business lowers the price so it can win the business.

You can tell a company that hasn't reached scale when they say, "We won't lose business because of price." That's a crazy statement. Of course, you might turn down business because the price is too low. If the price were $1, you'd probably turn it down.

That statement is another way of saying, "We don't really know how much we should charge, so let's just start a dialog about it." That statement has an air of desperation to it.

Companies that scale know their prices. They may choose to discount, but they do so strategically and according to a known set of rules.

The percentage of your price that goes to profit is called your profit margin. This profit margin percentage varies widely by industry. You should talk to people in your industry and find out what their profit margins are so you can set something similar.

Here are a few guidelines to help you price appropriately for profitability.

1. Include your regular salary in the operating expenses category. Don't pay yourself your base salary only when you're profitable. Otherwise, you won't have a sustainable business.

2. If your product or service requires you to take any risk (i.e., financing your customer's purchase or not getting paid if you're not successful), then your profit margin should be substantially higher than normal to reflect this risk.

3. The less unique your Value Proposition, the lower your profit margin will be. In other words, if your product is just like everyone else's, expect to have a lower profit margin. This lowering of profit margin is called "commoditization," because a product that is similar to every other one is a commodity.

4. Products and services that require unique knowledge or skill have higher profit margins, while products and services that are more like a manufacturing process have lower margins.

5. If you sell information-based or consultative-types of products and you have no idea how to price them, start with a 50% profit margin: double your expenses to set your price. See how the market responds, and adjust your strategy from there.

## Pricing for Availability

One part of pricing that is often overlooked by business owners is pricing according to your team's availability. In short, if your product or service involves resources that may be scarce (be they raw materials or your team's time), that should be reflected in your price, however this can be adjusted to reflect your desire to do a job or whether that particular work excites you.

Regardless of what it takes to produce the product – materials, time, or your own desire – if those materials are in short supply, your price should go up. That's the law of supply and demand.

You might think this is a joke, but it's not. Particularly for businesses that are moving away from an owner-centric service to a scalable product, there will be a transition period during which you, as the business owner, are still delivering your high-touch, non-scalable service while you're rolling out your new scalable, less time-intensive offering. During this transition period, your prices for your existing services should begin to increase.

Why? Because your time is now worth much more than the money you make on that original service offering. Your time should be used to dedicate yourself to scaling your business. Because of that, it's scarce.

You'll find that by continuing to raise your prices on your high-touch offering while you build a new product and platform, you will naturally wean yourself off those time-intensive endeavors. There is also a side benefit; because you will have choices, you can retain just those projects that actually are fun and rewarding for you, personally.

How far should you raise prices? There's no hard and fast rule, but it's reasonable for your prices to increase between 3%-7% on an annual basis, depending on your industry. Most business owners don't raise prices annually, and so you may have an increase due. If you find that you have to make a big price increase in order to "catch up" with the market, be respectful of your customers: give them plenty of warning, an honest explanation of the change, and listen for feedback.

If you are raising prices because you're slowly weeding out customers, be honest but tactful. There's no sense in telling people that you're getting rid of the trash, but don't make up a fake excuse to justify the increase. Simply explain that your time is limited, and by raising prices you can ensure that you're working with the clients that are most likely to get the highest return on their investment and can afford to pay you to spend the time with them that they need. Cast it in a positive light. Don't apologize. This is a good thing – for you, and ultimately for your customers.

## Pricing for Market Need

It's no surprise that the market responds differently to different prices. And it responds differently depending on what customers actually need and want at that particular moment. But in general, higher prices may mean higher profit, but it also means fewer sales.

One of the mistakes many business owners make is to price their services for marginal profitability. In other words, they ask, "How much profit will I make per customer?" But that's the wrong question to ask. The right question is: "How much profit will I make in total?"

Taking total profit into consideration means thinking not just about how much you should add onto the expenses to get the marginal profit, but also how many products you will actually sell.

Think about it this way: imagine you were pricing a book that cost you five dollars to produce. If you price for marginal profit, you might think: "I'll price the book at ten dollars, so I make five dollars per book." While that's true, consider this: at ten dollars per book, you may sell 500 copies, whereas at eight dollars per book you may sell 900 copies.

So what's better? Five dollars per book profit and selling 500 books, or only three dollars per book profit and selling 900?

In the first case, your total profit is $5 x 500 = $2500. In the second case, your total profit is $3 x 900 = $2700. So it looks like it makes sense to lower the price of the book to eight dollars because you make more money in total, even though you make less money on each individual book.

This pricing model takes price sensitivity into consideration. (Price sensitivity is a measure of the increased amount of product you sell because of a change in price — typically, by lowering the price.)

This isn't an economics class, so I won't go into the details, but the idea is to think not just about marginal profit but about total profit. Measuring price sensitivity and predicting exactly how much you should charge is complicated. It's the kind of calculations that airlines and hotels make every day. It's enough for you to keep in mind the broad principal: price for total profit, not just marginal profit.

The price sensitivity of your customers will change over time. As you become more well-known, sensitivity will decrease, meaning that your customers will tolerate paying more and more for your product. As you change target markets and start working with smaller businesses or lower-income consumers, price sensitivity will increase, meaning that you will see a steeper drop-off in purchases when you raise prices.

You should keep track of purchase data over time, especially if you are changing prices. If you have a large enough prospect base, it's not a bad idea to price test — occasionally change prices just to see what happens to purchase volumes. That way, you can start to understand how your prospects will react when your change prices and you can develop some ideas of the best price to charge.

The mathematics to find the right price using price sensitivity can be tricky, but here's a rule of thumb: if you increase your prices, say 5%

and it results in a decrease in sales of less than about 5%[1] then you can probably increase your price a little and still make more money. However, if you increase prices by 5% and it results in more than a 5% decrease in sales, you probably should lower prices a little to see if you can generate greater total profit.

---

[1] The real number is 4.76%, but these are all estimates anyways so an approximation is close enough.

## EXERCISE 9.1 APPROPRIATE PRICING

**Do this exercise with your product that produces the most revenue.**

1. List all the costs that go into delivering your product - the cost of goods sold (COGS). _____

_____

2. What is the operating expenses component of your product? Take your average monthly expenses and divide it by the portion you allocate to this product. _____

_____

3. What profit margin will you allocate to this product? Consider your need for profitability, your availability, and the market need. _____

_____

4. What will your final price be for this product? _____

# Chapter 10. Cash Flow Planning

## Cash Flow Formula

Money is one of the most difficult issues to deal with in business. And cash flow is like the pulse of your business. It is a measure of how well your business is doing. Go without cash and soon you won't have a business anymore.

When transitioning from one Business Model to another, one of the biggest problems you will face is cash flow. Change sometimes requires spending but not always, and getting that balance right can be tricky.

I was fortunate enough to speak with Sarah Thompson, creator of the More Money Mentoring program that helps small business owners manage their finances. We talked about cash flow and how to strike the right balance to keep money coming in and eventually getting your business flush with cash.

"Cash flow problems are one of three things. You either aren't selling enough, you're spending too much, or your timing is off," she says.

Money comes in; money goes out. When it does those two things are largely determined by you, the business owner. Now, unexpected things can happen, but more often than not, you are in complete control over the three components: not selling enough, spending too much, or timing being off.

Because the typical reader is likely a service-oriented business, I'm going to forgo discussions about companies that require a large physical inventory or need the products you sell to be manufactured in

China in order to sell economically. Those businesses still can apply many of these principles, but the investment required to generate and maintain an inventory is fundamentally different for service-oriented businesses or those that sell technology or information products.

Sarah says the goal she works for with her clients is to have a one-month savings buffer built up so that you are paying this month's bills with last month's money – including your payroll and owner's draw. If that sounds like a stretch, know that it comes over time. Working towards that buffer should be one of your first goals in cash flow planning.

Let's walk through both sides of your income statement – inflows and outflows – and talk about how to structure each for a financially healthy, scalable business.

## Borrowing and Investment

Money comes into your business through borrowing, investment, or sales. Let's tackle the first two quickly because they're often either out of reach or not applicable to most service-oriented businesses looking to change their Business Model.

Far too many business owners look to borrowing as a way to bridge cash flow gaps. Besides your personally funding your business – through deferred salaries or personal credit cards – Sarah says that, "The most common source of borrowed funds are the three F's: Friends, Family, and Fools." If you can convince these groups to give you money: great. Just keep in mind that repayment comes with conditions. If you can't meet those conditions, you may run into personal problems with those groups – well, maybe not with the fools.

When money is borrowed, you are required to pay back the amount, usually with interest. There is no promise of future profits or equity in your company: that would be an investment. When the principal and interest is paid back, the obligation is over.

The second common source of borrowed funds is from the owner's home equity. If you put up your home's equity in order to grow your business, keep in mind that you're putting your house at risk. If things go badly in the business and you can't pay yourself, you'll be not only defaulting on a loan that could cause the foreclosure of your home, but also deny your family the necessary funds to pay the original mortgage or find other accommodations (such a security deposit on an apartment) should you have to leave. It will also affect your credit rating.

Home equity is a very risky proposition, but these loans are probably the easiest to obtain, assuming that your credit is good and the value of your home minus any existing mortgage is big enough.

The third common source Sarah mentions are business loans from banks and other business lenders. These loans, however, commonly come with a personal guarantee from the owner. Although these loans may not put your home at risk, they may put your personal credit at risk. Be careful when personally guaranteeing any financing for your business. If things don't go well, you could ruin your credit right at the time you need to find a job. And that potential employer may check your credit as part of the employment process.

Bank loans are a tricky proposition for small business. The old joke goes, banks only lend money to businesses that don't need it. And if you need it, no bank will lend it to you.

It's only slightly an exaggeration as the tightening credit policies of banks across the globe have made us patently aware. Don't rely on borrowing as a way to fund your growing company unless you are large or have inventory or another major business asset to use as collateral.

Getting an investor for your business is not as easy as it once was. Long gone are the days when an entrepreneur with a dream and a good slide presentation could walk into an investor meeting and get money. The typical path for getting investors goes like this: first, friends and family; next, angel investors; and finally, venture capital. You don't have to take each step, but you rarely can jump ahead unless you're a repeat entrepreneur with a good track record of returning ten times or more of investors' money on a past deal.

In addition, investors have a hard time investing in service-oriented businesses. They usually don't see the opportunity to scale – exactly your problem if you're reading this book. Investors want to see that you are ready and able to grow. They need to know how their money will be returned to them ten-fold or even one hundred-fold.

If you can convince friends and family to invest in your business, keep in mind that you've just taken on a partner with whom you have a personal relationship. It could go badly, despite the allure of partnering with someone you like. And don't even think about asking for money from someone you don't like. If you don't like them when there is no money involved, you'll really hate them later.

Angel investors are wealthy business owners or former entrepreneurs who like to help small business succeed by putting some money at risk. It used to be that an angel might be interested in your business idea but that's rarely the case anymore. Angels are much more interested in seeing that you have a product or service with a few clients.

You might be able to talk an angel into investing in a business that is earning money in order to transition into another business, but usually they want to see the new idea tested on your own dime, with a few clients already booked, just to prove the concept.

Venture capitalists (or VCs), which used to be the first investment stop once you had a prototype product, now want to see some measure of success. VCs are interested in putting their money towards products that have a proven market and some track record of success but now need an influx of capital to fund sales and marketing efforts. This stage is usually a few years away for you at this point.

In short, borrowing and investing are usually bad ways to get money into your business. They take up a lot of the founder's time and are rarely successful. And when they are, they come with baggage that keeps you from achieving your business potential.

## Bootstrapping

All is not lost, however. There is another way to get money into your business: selling products.

Bootstrapping refers to using your own sales to finance your company's growth. It's a very popular method of growing a small business because technology and tools have become cheaper.

"The trick to bootstrapping," Sarah says, "is timing your growth."

And timing is the key.

There are two things you can time: your revenue and your spending. You probably need to do both.

You can accelerate revenue by rolling out a Minimum Viable Product, even if it's less than what you had hoped to create. I talked about this in an earlier chapter.

There are pricing models that can accelerate and smooth revenue. I talked about those in earlier chapters, too. Remember, you have created a concept that enables diverse, recurring, and stable income. So ask yourself, "How are you getting paid?"

You can either be paid in advance or in arrears – after you complete the work. Sarah explains: "There is just no reason anymore for you to be paid in arrears.

"Most business owners aren't paid in advance because they hesitate to ask for it," she says.

And if you think about it, you pay a lot of people in advance, or at least in real time. You can't see the doctor unless you make your co-pay first. Many businesses require you to pay up front, so why not you?

"The pricing and your payment terms go together," Sarah says. "You simply state, 'This is how I get paid.'"

I learned this lesson the hard way. Many years ago, I had a business that performed IT services for the transportation contractor of a major international sporting event. We had someone on-site delivering the service to whom we paid a salary on a regular basis during the planning phase and during the event, itself. The contractor asked to be billed after the event, when "things calmed down." I reluctantly (and mistakenly) agreed.

When the sporting event was over, the contractor rolled up and left town. The bill went out and thirty days later was still unpaid. When I called to find out why, I was told the owner had gone off to Greece on vacation and would likely not be back in the office for a month. No bills could be paid until he returned.

Cash had already been paid out to our employee and was not coming in from this customer. This put us in a severe cash flow crunch. It started to affect all our other clients. We had to cut back; sales and marketing slowed. It had a huge impact on our business.

Finally, after ninety days, I had had enough. I called the international sporting event sponsor and said that their transportation contractor had skipped town without paying their bills, and that if the situation wasn't resolved within an hour, I was going to the press to talk about how the international sporting event had been bad for local business.

Luckily, that struck a nerve, and within an hour the contractor had called me back. Complaining about the "quality of service" he received, he knuckled me down for a 50% discount. Desperate, I took it.

Imagine how much differently this situation would have gone if I had simply insisted on different payment terms.

You might argue, "I wouldn't have gotten the job at all." Maybe not. But maybe that would have been better than what actually happened.

The fact is, it doesn't matter. I've learned my lesson. Now I get paid in advance.

"Not accepting credit cards is another bad decision," Sarah explains. "No one likes paying the fee to the credit card companies, but by not accepting them, you make your potential customer delay their decision to buy. Many will just not come back. Plus, you lose out on the opportunity to have your money in two to three days. All over a few dollars? It's crazy."

Another way to encourage cash flow is to offer payment plans. A payment plan is a good idea when your offering is too much to reasonably expect from your target audience to pay upfront. Finding a good monthly plan that is affordable can entice your customer to spend more with you over time, in a regular way.

But be cautious when creating these plans. "It's all about understanding your risk tolerance," Sarah says. "If the person stops paying, what leverage do you have?"

I like to ask the question, "Can you shut it off?" That means: make sure that if the payment is still going on there is some benefits you can shut off so there is a penalty for non-payment.

In other words, if you have a six-month program, don't extend payments into month seven. This is a bad idea for two reasons. First, there is no incentive for your customer to make the seventh payment, and second, your customer's perception of the value of that seventh payment is very low.

Sure, they've just gotten financing and they should see it that way, but they usually don't. All they see is money going out for something they're not benefitting from anymore. Don't create this negative feeling unnecessarily in your customer's mind.

The best thing to do is to make sure the payments last only until the benefit has been achieved and no longer. If you have a twelve-month program, extend the payments for ten months. Or, if you have a training program in which the customer gets a video each week for five months, make sure the payments don't extend beyond five months, even if the customer has access to those videos for longer than that.

## Spending and Budgeting

Turning our attention to the spending side of the equation, you can time your spending by considering how much you need to spend to finance your growth. And with small, scalable businesses, you're really funding technology and people.

"Investigate your minimum viable options," Sarah suggests.

You may need a website, but do you need a $7000 website? You may need an office, but does it have to be rented?

You can do more with less these days; not only does this help your cash flow, but it helps you focus, as well. With more expenses, comes more maintenance. And more maintenance keeps you away from the things that really matter – earning revenue from customers.

"Spending too much is a common mistake," Sarah explains. "People think they have to do everything to do anything."

I see that problem all the time. You have to have a website to sell. And that website needs all the bells and whistles because, well, you might need them and you don't want to be caught without them.

A lot of business owners spend money investing in things so they "don't leave money on the table." I can't tell you how many times I've heard that from companies that aren't making any money. My response is that, "There isn't any money on the table to leave."

Go do something, then add as you go.

You can start with manually processing orders before you invest in automated order processing. Will it take you more time? Sure, but your time is only worth what you're earning. Hire someone to do the manual processing. That may be even cheaper in the short run.

"People invest in things way too early," Sarah notes. "It's the shiny object syndrome. People want to buy things before they're even ready to use them. Start with the free version of the software, and when it gets annoying, upgrade to the paid version."

My mantra is: spend on pain; don't spend in anticipation of the pain. Spend when the pain is happening because you may never experience the pain and that money won't come back to you.

Where entrepreneurs often get off track is in education. Think about how much you've spent on books, or learning, or programs. How many programs do you need? You probably can't absorb more than a few. If you're a perpetual learner, this will be a familiar problem.

I'll paraphrase Chris Ducker in a recent video posted to his Facebook group, Virtual Freedom Alliance: "Stop it!" Chris' advice is to stop all the *learning* and start *doing*. That will cut down on expenses and improve your revenue timing.

What about those "surprise expenses?"

Sarah says, "Is it really a surprise?" Her point is: did you not know it was coming?

"Taxes are not a surprise. Put money away for taxes. Put aside some money each month to get a new computer because you're going to eventually need a new computer," she adds.

Even if it's not something scheduled, you should be able to anticipate most surprise expenses. Other surprises, such as not getting paid, can be handled by how you structure your terms. It's a matter of having a budget and sticking with it.

"Budgeting is just spending less than you make," Sarah says. "You need to know your minimum budget: your 'nut,' as I like to call it. Know how much you need to support yourself and your business expenses, today and in the future."

Sarah suggests using some technology to help with this. "My clients use software to help them bucket their money into categories. That way they know exactly how much they should spend on different areas of their business. Also, make sure one expense doesn't end up cannibalizing another," she explains. In other words, if you've budgeted $100 for office supplies, don't spend an extra $100 on business lunches or that $100 won't be there when you need it.

If this is an area you're uncomfortable with, then get help. Find a mentor or coach that can help you develop your budget. It is worth the investment.


Cash flow is the sign of your business' health. If you have negative or low cash flow, you will likely not be in business for very long. Lack of cash flow is one of the biggest reasons why companies go out of business.

You manage cash flow by managing the components: inflows, outflows, and timing. Find ways to accelerate sales. Know your 'nut.' Make sure you're paying your vendors after the money comes in. Each of these pieces will build a strong cash flow pipeline that will continue to build your business strength over time.

## EXERCISE 10.1 CASH FLOW PLANNING

1. How are you being paid today? In advance? In arrears? Outline the payment terms of your largest expected product. _____

_____

_____

_____

_____

_____

2. Think of two ways you can accelerate your monetization? How can you go to market more quickly with a minimum product? _____

_____

_____

_____

_____

_____

3. What is your 'nut?' What is your minimum monthly budget requirement, including your salary, draw, and regular business expenses? _____

_____

_____

_____

_____

4. List your biggest expenses - besides your salary and draw. Estimate their monthly expense. _____

_____

_____

_____

# Section 4. The Market

# Chapter 11. Building Loyalty

## What is the Loyalty Ladder?

The Loyalty Ladder is, in my opinion, the most important tool you have when planning your marketing execution. The best way to talk about the Loyalty Ladder is to start with an example.

Let's build a Loyalty Ladder for a B2B business whose customers are other business owners. We're going to create a series of campaigns that helps your prospect identify how they move from one need segment to the next.

We'll start off with an initial opt-in of some kind. The Loiterer needs to be educated about what you do. Let's say we do that with a newsletter. The newsletter is the value we add to the prospect, and in exchange we get some contact information.

When prospects are ready to become Lookers, they need another Value Proposition from us. So, let's say we offer some kind of client educational program. We, of course, create the client education in order to paint the vision of the One Big Result we provide. Our prospects can see that One Big Result in their own lives as a result of this client education program.

In exchange, we engage with a prospect and really understand their wants and preferences. Perhaps we ask a few introductory questions to deepen our engagement with the prospect. This is a low-risk value exchange. The swap of information for education should be acceptable for our prospect.

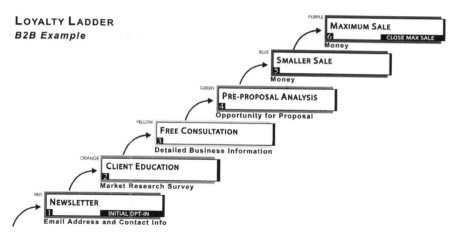

*Figure 3. The Loyalty Ladder*

Now, our prospect is ready to move on to start to understand the specifics of our offer. What better way to engage with our business owner than to offer some initial, free consultation. Many people do not like free consultations because they can waste time and cheapen the value of our product or service, but we've been careful not to lead with this offer, instead putting it behind a few gatekeeping campaigns to ensure that our prospect is ready and qualified.

Having said all of that, there's no reason why a free consultation is the only thing we can offer here. Perhaps, we can deploy software or a smart-survey that asks the questions we would and provides general consultative advice based on the answers. That is a scalable way of personalizing your Value Proposition. I see that often in the form of value calculators, needs-based assessments, or expert product selection systems.

But what's the value exchange for us? Part of that interaction is a scoping and discovery effort. We're asking questions, getting answers, and saving those answers to use later. Even if they do not pay for this session, we're getting something of value: information to personalize an offer.

If we've done this consultation well, our prospect will want to receive a proposal. Good proposals will also be a value to the prospect because they inform them and outline the forward path. They explain and justify the investment and describe in detail how your One Big Result will drive value in their business.

This opportunity is very valuable to us because it's the chance to convert a prospect into a Customer. Because our prospect is a Buyer at this stage, our proposal needs to outline every step they need to take in order to transact business. Thus, we fulfill the need of the Buyer: knowing how to transact business with us.

Hopefully, from here we can execute a sale. Usually, a first time customer buys our "smaller offer." The value we get is money. This value exchange is what it's all about.

Think carefully about having multiple offers. Many companies have a small sale and a bigger sale. Sometimes the bigger sale is simply multiple purchases. Either way, you should have a path to capitalize on existing Customers.

Now, we have a Customer. We provide Information, Service, and Support in exchange for Customer loyalty. If we execute a customer satisfaction survey, resolve any concerns, and provide incentives, our Customer will become a Fan.

Fans generate more revenue, either through their own efforts or by purchasing more.


This was just an example, but you can see some broad principles. We'll discuss those shortly, but before I get to that, I want to mention something about exchanging money. You can decide anywhere in this Loyalty Ladder to exchange money. You could sell client education if you want. That doesn't really change need segment definitions because you're still educating prospects. Just ensure you have an *even value exchange* if you ask for money.

## Building Your Loyalty Ladder

Now that we've talked about what a Loyalty Ladder is, let's spend some time discussing what it takes to build your own. There are four sets of rules to follow when building your Loyalty Ladder. These rules will make sure your Loyalty Ladder is effective and efficient.

Rule 1: Your Loyalty Ladder has to contain a campaign of every color.

That means no skipping need segments. Your prospect has to make the journey through every need segment, from Loiterer to Looker, Shopper, Buyer, Customer, and hopefully into Fan. If you do not explicitly create the conditions for those to occur, your prospect will have to do it themselves, if they do it at all.

So you need one for each segment. Think through the Value Proposition you can offer to each need segment. Remember that for the lower stages that Value Proposition doesn't have to be much — maybe just an explanation of the One Big Result you create. But there needs to be value at every stage.

Rule 2: The campaigns have to go in order.

Each campaign increases based on the need segment, in order. At the top, you provide the biggest benefit you offer: your One Big Result. How you get to the top is up to you, but increase the value you offer as you go up the need segments. And you'll want to align the offer with the level of engagement for each segment.

It seems obvious that you would want a campaign focused on Lookers to come first and campaigns focused on Buyers to come next, but you'd be surprised how often companies get this wrong.

For example, I recall one bank's website that had a big button labeled "Apply Now" for a loan. When you clicked that button, it led you to a series of pages that educated you about the kind of loan you were applying for and why you would want that kind of loan.

I call that kind of mistake "de-migration." You do not want to de-migrate prospects by putting a Looker campaign after a Buyer campaign. Go in order.

Rule 3: Provide an even value exchange for each campaign.

As I mentioned earlier, your earlier campaigns do not have to offer too much. They can simply offer an explanation, or some training video, or something else that doesn't require your personal involvement. But on the other hand, you'll get something of lesser value for it.

For training, you might exchange personal information. For a personal quote or other personalized engagement, you'll need something more from the prospect. Maybe you'll want to learn more about their life or business so you can personalize your offering.

But in each case, the value of what you get should equal the value of what you give. You can't say, "We're going to provide you some blog posts" and then expect your prospect to pay for them. That's not an even value exchange.

On the flip side, you also don't want to make the opposite mistake, which is to give away more than you're asking in return. In other words, you don't want to do a free consultation and never collect any of that information and use it later to try and sell.

The value doesn't have to be money, but it does have to be of value to you.

Rule 4: As you collect information, think ahead. Collect what will facilitate future campaigns.

This rule is the connective tissue between campaigns. If you collect contact information in your first campaign, make sure you need it for the second campaign. If you learn about someone's life or business in the second campaign, make sure you need it for the third.

That kind of coordination requires some planning. Think about what you need — and only what you need — to transact business and work backwards. Spread that information across a few campaigns and make sure you need it at every stage.

If you need something, don't hesitate to ask for it. Just make sure you have something of equal value to exchange.

One last comment about building your own Loyalty Ladder: your Loyalty Ladder will not be static; it's going to change. That means as you put it in place, make sure you leave it flexible for feedback and learning.

It's always good to have a mentor or mastermind group to run ideas past. They can help you fill holes and pressure-test your ideas to make sure you're covering all your bases.

This help is especially important in testing your value exchanges. Outside eyes can often see if you're asking too much or leaving too much of a gap between campaigns.

### Summary of the Rules

1. Your Loyalty Ladder must contain a campaign of every color for every need segment.

2. The campaigns must go in order.

3. Provide an even value exchange for each campaign.

4. As you collect information, think about what you will need in future campaigns.

## EXERCISE 11.1 BUILDING YOUR OWN LOYALTY LADDER

1. Create a Value Proposition - an offering - for each need segment:

A. The Fan: (your maximum sale) _____

B. The Customer: (your smaller sale) _____

C. The Buyer: (your pre-sale offer) _____

D. The Shopper: (your "get the facts" offer) _____

E. The Looker: (your "catch the vision" offer) _____

F. The Loiterer: (your education offer) _____

2. Follow rule #3: make sure it's an even value exchange.

Go through each offering and see if it's reasonable for your need segment.

3. Follow rule #4: think about what information you need to deliver the Value Proposition in each stage. What information do you need to deliver each offering?

A. The Fan offering: _____

B. The Customer offering: _____

C. The Buyer: _____

D. The Shopper: _____

E. The Looker: _____

F. The Loiterer: _____

# Chapter 12. Marketing & Advertising Campaigns

## The Difference between Marketing & Advertising

Now that you've build your own Loyalty Ladder we can talk about the difference between marketing and advertising. I'm sure that business schools have set definitions, but for our purposes, we're going to define them in a very particular way.

Marketing is what you do to encourage prospects to move up the Loyalty Ladder.

Advertising is what you do to feed new people into the Loyalty Ladder.

From here on, when I refer to marketing, I'm talking about prospects migrating up the chain to become Customers. Advertising will be focused on attracting new prospects onto the Loyalty Ladder at some stage. Keep in mind that advertising might drive prospects right into the Buyer phase where they have their credit cards out.

You need to have a marketing campaign for each stage of the Loyalty Ladder. That's not the case for advertising. You will choose one or more stages at which you want people to join the Loyalty Ladder. We'll talk later about how you make that determination, but for now, know that we'll be picking and choosing.

## The Four Calls-to-Action

One basic question you may be asking yourself is: How do I know which message to use for a marketing or advertising campaign?"

That's the right question to ask. The wrong message will overpower good design, the right channel, and even a great value exchange.

The answer, of course, is, "it depends." It depends on the need segment of your prospect. But there are really only four basic types of calls-to-action. You can change the language based on what you think motivates the prospect. In addition, research shows that phrasing the call-to-action as an imperative or command works well.

## *"Buy Now"*

The most direct and common call-to-action is the one that expects the prospect to whip out their wallet: "Buy Now!"

You can see "Buy Now" phrased different ways in different product areas. On an e-commerce catalog, that call-to-action may first just say, "Add to Cart." But fundamentally, we're asking the prospect to buy the item that they're adding to their cart.

Other times, "Buy Now" may be phrased in terms of the product you're interested in buying. Such as "Become a Member" or "Build My Plan." This type of wording is much more relevant and specific to the situation and can lift response by personalizing the request.

Sometimes "Buy Now" doesn't involve money, but instead requires the prospect to get started with the product for free. This variation is common among "freemium" Business Models – products that have a free trial period or a money-back guarantee.

In all of these cases, the "Buy Now" call-to-action is directed at a prospect ready to commit. Depending on your product or service, this may take some time to develop. In the case of e-commerce, often the user can go from Loiterer to Buyer very quickly, so an "Add to Cart" and "Purchase Cart" makes sense.

But sometimes, you need to build trust with your prospect and a "Buy Now" call-to-action is too much, too soon. Instead, build a marketing strategy that builds trust first, and then follow with the "Buy Now" call-to-action.

## *"Fix It"*

Before a prospect is ready to buy, they often just want to fix their problems, which of course, may encourage them to buy. The "Fix It" call-to-action is geared towards making your prospect's problem go away.

Quick Sprout has a great "Fix It" call-to-action on their home page. They identify the problem: you don't have enough traffic. Want to fix it? Then sign up.

The "Fix It" call-to-action can lead to a sale, but more often it precedes it. The Shopper knows what his or her problem is and wants it fixed. Any language that encourages him or her to fix that problem qualifies.

It's a strong call-to-action and can often be used to figure out what kind of prospect you have and how best to help them.

*Figure 4. QuickSprout Call-To-Action*

Often, "Fix It" calls-to-action come in groups with the prospect choosing the one that is aligned with their need. Here, the marketing strategy is to sort prospects by need segments so you can point them in the direction of the right solution.

But not all prospects have identified their problem. If a Prospect is learning about your company, but hasn't yet decided if they have the pain you're trying to alleviate, then they may need a different call-to-action.

## *"Better Life"*

This call-to-action is the one most familiar to us on TV commercials. Because you are not likely to get up from your couch and buy something immediately, most big brands try to make you feel better about buying their product – when you finally get around to it.

Think of almost every beer commercial you've ever seen. You'll be sexier, have more friends, richer . . . you get the idea.

Sure, the "Better Life" is solving a problem; it's just not one you've identified yet. The marketing strategy here is to simply brand a product as creating a better life – whatever that means for your perfect customer.

So, this call-to-action is focusing on your felt needs: something you need, but haven't verbalized or even thought about yet. It operates at an emotional level.

The Looker responds best to the "Better Life" call-to-action because they want what you're offering – even if they didn't know they wanted it before they met you. It's a critical way to help your prospect identify their need – even if it's not spoken.

Don't think this call-to-action is only useful in TV advertising; it's also critical in direct marketing. If our prospect doesn't immediately know or believe that they have the need you're addressing, you'll have to show how your product or service will create a better life. Depending on how effectively you can convince your prospect that you can provide that better life, you may have a "Get a Stress-Free Life" or "Have More Spending Money" call-to-action. This is the direct marketer's equivalent of the beer commercial.

## "Learn More"

The very first call-to-action in any marketing strategy to even the most unqualified prospect is "Learn More."

This basic invitation is designed to be the lowest level of commitment you can ask of a prospect – simply to spend some time to find out more.

The "Learn More" call-to-action is also one of the most commonly used online strategies to get prospects to provide information. All of content marketing is essentially a "Learn More" strategy.

Any free offer that teaches your prospect something they didn't know before is a "Learn More" call-to-action. It may be phrased in relation to the thing you're teaching. For example, CrazyEgg's website says "Show Me My HeatMap," which actually teaches their prospect something new they didn't know before.

The Loiterer responds only to "Learn More" calls-to-action because they don't know what you're business is about yet. Keep in mind that your prospect is responding because they really do want to learn something, so don't hide sales material behind a "Learn More" call-to-action. If you think your prospect is ready to buy, then give them a "Buy Now" or a "Fix It" call-to-action that is in line with their expectations.

## When to Use Each

Obviously, there are a million different variations of each of these campaigns, but calls-to-action speak to prospects in very specific ways.

The Buyer responds to the "Buy Now" call-to-action because it answers his or her fundamental question, "How do I get this product?" then the "Buy Now" call-to-action should be the last one you use. What's not as clear is that it should rarely be the first.

One big mistake companies make in marketing language is to rush into a sales conversation before the prospect is ready. The "Buy Now" call-to-action is the final tool at our disposal to engage. Use it wisely.

The Shopper responds to the "Fix It" call-to-action because he or she has a pain point; something hurts and it needs to be fixed. The Shopper is keenly aware of his or her needs and hopes you have the answer. Often companies use the "Fix It" call-to-action but fail to follow up with a "Buy Now" call-to-action. It's important you help your prospect make the transition.

The Looker responses to the "Better Life" call-to-action because he or she is curious. By the time a prospect becomes a Looker, he or she is ready to see the vision. This call-to-action paints that picture and can be extremely compelling. It's important to remember that this call-to-action isn't enough to get a sale. In the vast majority of cases, you will still need to make a case that your product or service fixes a problem. In other words, the Looker needs to turn into a Shopper, and you will have to engage facts and figures. Vision may start the conversation, but it rarely concludes it.

The Loiterer can only respond to the "Learn More" call-to-action because you haven't yet earned anything more from them. Generally speaking, "Learn More" will be the first call-to-action you use, but don't let it be the last. You will need to identify problems and fix them in order to convert your prospect to Customer. A mistake salespeople often make is thinking that by helping a Loiterer learn more about their product's features, they can make a sale. Remember that once a prospect becomes a Shopper, they are no longer interested in learning for learning's sake; they have a problem and they want a solution. Make sure you provide one.

## Creating Advertising & Marketing Copy

What's the purpose of our marketing and advertising copy? Simple. It's to drive prospects onto or up through the Loyalty Ladder.

When we write marketing copy, we know exactly which need segment we're speaking to: Loiterer, Looker, Shopper, or Buyer. When we write advertising copy, we're going out to essentially an anonymous prospect base and we're trying to bring them to the Loyalty Ladder.

But that doesn't mean we have to muddle our message. We can still choose a need segment to speak to in that mass crowd. The ones who respond to our call-to-action will self-select as Loiterer, Looker, Shopper, or Buyer. Then we can react accordingly.

Let's start with advertising copy. First, we have to answer the question: into which level is the campaign going to insert prospects? Once we've decided what that is, then we can craft messaging and a call-to-action that fits the audience.

Make sure whatever you're directing the prospect to do, the "other end of the line," whoever picks up the phone or reads the form response or whatever, is ready to engage in a conversation that matches the need segment.

This is probably the biggest mistake people make in advertising. They setup a "Learn More" call-to-action that sends the prospect to a "hard sell" campaign. Total mismatch.

Sometimes, it's even worse. A business creates a "Buy Now" campaign that sends the prospect to someone who wants to setup a tour. Why bother? Your prospect has reacted to "Buy Now." Take their money.

It's easy to get this wrong on the internet, but it happens most often when call center representatives and sales executives use a script which doesn't adjust to the campaign to which the prospect is responding.

Your staff in call centers needs to be trained. Use different toll-free numbers for different campaigns, and make sure the staff knows who they're talking to so they can assess migration signals from their prospects.

Your landing pages need to match. If you have a "Learn More" advertising campaign that directs people to a landing page, the content of that page needs to be directed to Loiterers. Don't send them to a shopping cart.

And of course, salespeople need to do the same thing. As they are interacting with prospects who are responding to an advertising campaign, they also need to know the language they should be speaking. What need segment does this prospect belong to?

## Internet as a Strategy

The internet is one of the most important tools for your marketing purposes. For most companies, your company website should serve as the nexus of your entire sales and marketing efforts. It's also the one most misused. Knowing what you know about need segments and Loyalty Ladders, you should be able to craft an internet strategy that aligns with your marketing.

First, you should ask yourself about every page: what is the goal of this page? What is the audience? What am I asking them to do?

You should know the answer to the last question. You want prospects to advance up the Loyalty Ladder. Now the only thing you need to know is: where is the prospect now?

When you have written down exactly how you want the migration path to look for your prospects, you have everything you need to know about what should be on your website. There shouldn't be anything else on there that doesn't fit into the communication plan.

You should see on your site map exactly what the migration path looks like. If you're not clear when people go from Loiterer to Looker or from Shopper to Buyer, no one else will either. It's important you spend the time to map this out correctly.

Every need segment should have some kind of content, especially on the homepage. On the second-level pages and your landing pages, it's a different story. But publicly available pages, such as your home page, will attract a varied audience. You should be prepared with content that helps prospects self-select based on their need segment.

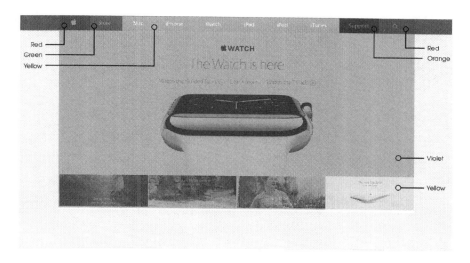

*Figure 5. Apple.com Home Page Color Coding*

Be consistent in your language. If you're using links with a "Buy Now" call-to-action, the linked page should have "Buy Now" content. Don't mismatch links with content by sending prospects to content that isn't for them.

Have one – and only one – link for each need segment. If you're trying to capture Lookers, do not give them seven places to click. Give them one really big "Better Life" call-to-action. If you have blog content, give them one place to click to get to your blog. If you have product selection software or an expert selection system embedded in your website, that's "Fix It" type of content. Provide one link to get there per page.

Don't give people multiple choices; they get confused. Customers and Prospects can easily tell what they're not, but if you give them five choices of what they are, they can get confused. Overabundance of choice is not a good thing.

Do an actual physical color coding of your homepage using red, orange, yellow, green, blue, and purple to see how well – and how much – you're speaking to each of the need segments. It's a great exercise to see, visually, how your home page reads to each need segment.

## Content Marketing as a Strategy

You can't talk about marketing these days without discussing content marketing. Content marketing can play an important role in driving prospects up the Loyalty Ladder.

In fact, that's its main goal. But since content remains on your website for others to see, it can also act as an advertising vehicle. Once they consume your content, we can use it to build a closer relationship.

Typically, content marketing splits into a couple of different areas: blogging and e-mail marketing.

Blogging is generally focused on your Loiterer crowd. A blog is just a large "Learn More" call-to-action. You're educating your prospect and building a relationship. But every blog should have an opt-in which encourages people to provide their contact information.

Keep in mind that every blog post should clearly include a reference to your target market and One Big Result. Any blog post could be read by anyone, and you want to make sure you are communicating effectively.

Another major content marketing strategy is the autoresponder. Your autoresponder will send out a series of e-mails to a prospect. The information in the e-mails is intended to migrate your Loiterer to a Looker. Will the autoresponder with "Better Life" calls-to-action encourage prospects to self-select when they migrate up the Loyalty Ladder?

If prospects react to one of these calls-to-action, they are immediately re-classified as Lookers and obtain different content. If your autoresponder program can handle it, shift the prospect to a new series of e-mails with Looker content.

Generally, the hardest part of the marketing process is the jump from Looker to Shopper. Once your prospect has become a Shopper, your content marketing strategy will start to take a back seat. It's very difficult to be consultative through an autoresponder. You will likely have to direct the prospect to another channel.

For high value sales, one thing I've seen that's quite good is the bounce from autoresponder to phone consultation. There are two really good ways to do this: free consultations, and prospect qualifiers.

First, you can simply tell your prospect that you offer free consultations, and if they're interested in working with you to schedule an appointment. Offer an online appointment scheduler and have the prospect fill out information to prepare you for the call.

Many people don't like free consultations; they feel it cheapens the value of their work. That certainly can be the case if you're not careful about how selective you are in offering it. You should make your prospect do a little upfront work before getting on the phone with them. In addition, you might consider dropping the word "consultation" and replacing it with "discovery session." That is much less likely to be confused with your main offering.

Alternatively, I've seen a very clever technique in bouncing people from autoresponder to phone call. I call it the "qualifier." If you have a high-value offering and you want to talk with people directly and sell them into the program, you can offer to talk to prospects see if they qualify for your program. This method works best if you follow these rules:

First, make sure you have an offer with real scarcity. In other words, you can only accept fifteen people or you can only work with five clients.

Second, provide a very brief phone call appointment. Provide enough time to get to know the person and ask for the sale because lack of time works to sell scarcity: "We're talking with a lot of people."

Third, pre-qualify everyone up front with a questionnaire that makes the prospect check a box that lets them know, upfront, the price of the service they're considering. That way, when you get to the sales conversation, the question of price is no longer relevant. In other words, you want the prospect to agree to the statement, "I know there is an investment of $1000 per month and I am willing to invest that if this is a good fit."

This technique is advanced and can go badly if not done properly, but I have seen it be particularly effective in generating high-value sales from a list.

For lower value sales, you will want automated systems and shopping carts. Hopefully, if the price is low, you can help people through the Shopper phase quickly. Either way, be smart about how much effort you spend to convert prospects for low-value products. Is there a strategy to monetize later?

## Sales as a Strategy

One last technique I want to address is direct, human sales. Obviously, a salesperson can be a marketing campaign. Typically, salespeople interact with known prospects, thus sales is marketing, not advertising.

When should you use sales in your Loyalty Ladder? There are two general principles to follow: timing and money.

Salespeople are typically engaged later in the sales process. By the time the prospect is a Shopper, they are generally ready to engage with a salesperson for high-ticket purchases (and even medium-ticket purchases.)

Loiterer and Lookers generally don't interact well with ordinary salespeople (remember, "I'm just looking"?). Lookers can interact well with tour guides and more visual, concierge-like staff, but if salespeople take the typical sales tack with Lookers, they generally do not succeed.

The second point is that salespeople are expensive. A rule of thumb is that salespeople should bring in at least ten times their salary in sales, maybe more. If the revenue generated by your campaign cannot support that Value Proposition, then you should consider another way of driving prospects to a sale.

And don't make the mistake of substituting yourself, as owner, for the salesperson. Even if your economics are different, if you build in a manual process for converting prospects, you will eventually have to make good on your threat – by hiring someone to handle the manual process. If the numbers don't work out today, they certainly won't work out in the future. The salesperson Value Proposition is a marginal one; it doesn't get better with volume.

If you have human being interact with prospects, it's critical that they know their role in the process. Are they interacting with Loiterers, Lookers, Shoppers, or Buyers? They should be able to know the difference and communicate accordingly.

Salespeople interacting with Buyers should focus on the logistics of completing the sale; they should not have to justify the sale. Often when Buyers are interacting with salespeople for the first time, the salesperson feels they have to justify the sale. But remember, the Buyer is "already there." The salesperson just needs to facilitate the transaction.

Have you ever felt like a salesperson was stalling the actual sale? I know it's crazy, but it happens. Make sure your salespeople recognize Buyers and handle them accordingly.

Shoppers need the classic salesperson touch. A consultative salesperson will find out the prospect's needs and identify the benefits that meet those needs. This mode is the natural mode for most salespeople; they do their best work with Shoppers.

Lookers, on the other hand, are trickier. A common mistake salespeople make with Lookers is trying move into consultative mode too quickly. They try to prequalify, or do a needs analysis; the Looker is not ready for those questions. First, the Looker doesn't yet know their needs, so asking them about what they need is premature. But more importantly, you haven't earned enough trust with the Looker to start engaging them in-depth. Wait until the trust level is higher and they migrate to Shopper.

So, what do salespeople do with Lookers? They tell stories. Not just random testimonials or case studies, but stories that focus on life with your product. Before and After shots give prospects a good sense of the "why" behind what you sell. You want your Looker thinking about the future and putting themselves in that spot.

Finally, salespeople should handle Loiterers the same way greeters handle people coming into a store. They are friendly, kind, and informative. Here, salespeople should quickly describe your target market and One Big Result. After the prospect agrees that they "belong," the salesperson should inform the Loiterer how they can learn more and set them on that path.

Human beings are extremely effective in the sales process. Where it makes sense, you should use them. But it's critical that each salesperson understand their role in the process and how to make it work. We'll explore this in more detail in Section 5.

## EXERCISE 12.1 MARKETING CAMPAIGNS

Describe the marketing campaign intended to migrate your prospects from one level to the next. Include the channel you would use and the call-to-action.

A. Loiterer to Looker: (description) _____

_____

Channel: _____

Call-to-Action: ("Learn More") _____

B. Looker to Shopper: (description) _____

_____

Channel: _____

Call-to-Action: ("Better Life") _____

C. Shopper to Buyer: (description) _____

Channel: _____

Call-to-Action: ("Fix It") _____

D. Buyer to Customer: (description) _____

_____

Channel: _____

Call-to-Action: ("Buy Now") _____

E. Customer to Fan: (description) _____

Channel: _____

Call-to-Action: ("Share the Love") _____

## EXERCISE 12.2 ADVERTISING CAMPAIGNS

In each case, describe the advertising campaign (if any) you would use to feed new prospects into the Loyalty Ladder. Including the channel you will use and the call-to-action. Note: you do not have to have an advertising campaign at every level. In fact, that would likely be counterproductive. You must have one, but more than one is dependent on your product and market.

A. Feeding Loiterers: (description) _____

Channel: _____

Call-to-Action: ("Learn More") _____

B. Feeding Lookers: (description) _____

Channel: _____

Call-to-Action: ("Better Life") _____

C. Feeding Shoppers: (description) _____

Channel: _____

Call-to-Action: ("Fix It") _____

D. Feeding Buyers: (description) _____

Channel: _____

Call-to-Action: ("Buy Now") _____

# Chapter 13. Managing Metrics

## Importance of Metrics

If there's one secret of marketing I can share with you, it's this: whatever you do the first time is not going to work; it's not going to work with way you think it's going to work and you're going to need to change.

But the changes you need to make require you to know where, when, how, and how much you should change. You will only know this if you are measuring your campaign and your audience's reaction to that campaign.

One of the mistakes people make when they start looking at marketing is thinking marketing is an "art," that it's something you have to "feel." But it is really a science with a quantitative component. This applies whether you're a large corporation or a small businesses. Even a small business must use quantitative tools to measure results.

You don't have to be a math expert to do this; I'm going to walk you through a couple of metrics that you'll need to be able to calculate and track with website and CRM (Customer Relationship Management) software that you should be able to get for your small business.

But if you don't have it, if you don't track it, then you're never going to know if it's working. The question that you're going to ask and be able to answer from all of this is: am I wasting my money on marketing? How much is it actually costing to get a new customer in the door? That's probably one of the most important questions you need to be able to answer, so we're going to talk about some of the necessary metrics in this section.

But remember back to the Loyalty Ladder; we built it this way on purpose. You've got all of the rules around the Loyalty Ladder; you've got campaigns of every color, and one leads to the next, but it's this infrastructure that's going to make it possible for us to manage what you're doing well.

We're going to take this as an example and measure where things go in and out of this Loyalty Ladder, There are two directions that are important to us: in and up.

People have to enter the Loyalty Ladder somewhere; maybe they all come in on step one, but maybe they come in on step three. Some people enter directly on step five, but they enter at some stage. And then, of course, we want them, regardless of where they start, to go up. Not everyone is going to go up, and not everyone's going to come in, but we need to measure those two things; those are the key elements we'll focus on.

We've talked a little bit already about how management is going to be the key to the success of your marketing campaign because whatever you do first is not going to work; it's going to require some changes. And in order to understand what those changes need to be, you must collect certain data.

For example, we've already talked about obtaining prospect and client contact information as part of a really good campaign. We need to know where each prospect or client is on the Loyalty Ladder at every moment. You should be able to open up a database or a report that's created for you that shows you how many Lookers there are, how many Loiterers there are, how many are in each area, and be able to identify them directly. We need to be able to measure how efficient the process is at moving prospects from one stage to the next, because that identifies what helps people who come in at lower stages make their way up to higher stages when they become worth more to us.

And, of course, we need to measure how quickly that happens. If it takes ten years to get from red to purple, maybe that's okay or maybe it's not, but you ought to adjust your price to that and understand that it's going to take ten years.

And we need to know which campaigns actually facilitated the migration and which did not. Some of those are going to be helpful, some are not; you need to pull out the ones that aren't working and replace them with ones that are. So being able to understand the migration process and understand which campaign actually made it happen is going to be very important.

Our feeder campaigns are the things that are coming in. These are our advertising campaigns, and we need to know how effective they are. Can we go out, blast our message to a large audience, and bring in lots of people, or are we cherry picking? And if so, how much money are we spending to do that? How much money does it cost us to get a new prospect onto the Ladder?

We also need to know how quickly prospects are going to respond. So if we do an advertising campaign to pull people in, how long does it take to get results – two days or a week? Regardless of the answer, we need to know these things.

These are the key data elements that we need to be able to collect and store. There are seven elements, and you need some way to collect and analyze them.

In order to do that, we need to encourage identification. That means creating the value exchange necessary to encourage the prospect to tell us who they are. (Please, by all means, keep the information private. Yes, you should have a privacy policy, and no, you should never sell your list to a third party – ever.)

You can get more information along the way if you ask, but start off with the basic, non-intrusive details; as people migrate and engage more with your business and build more trust, you can ask for more 'personal' information, but this is primarily information that valuable to you in the sales process.

With each transaction, always provide an incentive for the individual to identify themselves. On the web, this is easy because people log in and have memberships, but in your store, loyalty cards, which have been used by grocery stores for a long time, do this. Loyalty cards capture what people are buying so you know who's buying what, how often they're coming in, and – this is very important – they are incented with savings to identify themselves.

The most important thing that you need to think through is that what you're tracking. We're looking at the outcome, not the activity, itself, so it's not enough to just track information. It's not enough to track visitors; you don't need to track how many eyeballs there were. Since it doesn't matter if people come to your website, why track it? What you want to track is whether they interacted with you. Did they click on something? Did they go where you wanted them to go on the website? As we talked about earlier, your web strategy needs to be full of migration paths, and those migration paths need to be very clear to you and very clear to the user. When somebody goes from A to B and clicks the link that indicates a migration signal, that's what you want to track. You don't want to track how many sales calls were made; you want to track outcomes.

## Response Rates and Migration Rates

### Response Rates

One of the most important metrics you need to calculate is the Response Rate. This rate tracks responses to your advertising campaigns: your feeder campaigns. Typically, these measurements are anonymous because you're advertising to a large group of people; you don't know them. We track when they respond to your advertising campaign. The ratio of responses to the total audience exposed to the ad is the response rate.

Many advertising campaigns today track the click, itself, rather than whether the user was exposed to the ad. In these cost-per-click campaigns, we don't really care about the original response rate because we don't pay for the traffic that the Customer sees but does not interact with. We only start paying when the first "click" comes in. That click is the first action that gets a prospect into the bottom of our Loyalty Ladder.

Remember that you're calculating cost-per-click rather than cost-per-view. Newspapers and web display ads are often priced based on cost-per-view. Google AdWords, Facebook ads, and LinkedIn ads can be priced on a cost-per-click basis.

What about when the "click" isn't an electronic one? If someone is responding to an offline ad, it can be difficult to determine the source of the lead. In order to estimate response rates, we use promotional codes, special toll-free numbers, or discount codes. The use of such a code should be tracked in your CRM database. If you encourage people to go online, you can use a campaign-specific web page addres or URL. These URLs make tracking easier.

Again, the main thing we're trying to calculate is the percentage of people who responded to a particular message. That ratio needs to be specific to the message. Each message will have a separate response rate.

Along with response rate, speed of response is important, as well. We need to measure the average time between campaign start and response. Average response time will be one of the critical metrics we use to understand our audience and effectiveness of our advertising campaign.

Whatever that number is today, it will change. It will move and flow with the market. It will move and flow with your messaging. You need to measure it frequently and consistently in order to understand how your market and message affect response rates. When that numbers starts to fall off, you know something in your market or message has changed and it's time for you to make a change.

## *Migration Rates*

The next metric you need to measure is the migration rate. This one is a bit different from the response rate. In fact, you may have never heard of it. The idea behind the migration rate is to track movement through the Loyalty Ladder. This rate measures the percentage of prospects that move from one stage of the Loyalty Ladder to the next.

Since we've collected information about your prospect upon entering the Loyalty Ladder, you can begin tracking that prospect's interaction with you. They are no longer anonymous. This is something you can track over time at the individual level. For example, you want to calculate the percentage of Lookers who eventually become Shoppers. Migration rates will also change over time. Measuring this rate will require you to track each number by stage in the Loyalty Ladder and keep track of its effectiveness. If you can, you should automate processes so you have a daily recalculation of migration rates. When a particular campaign stops working, you will be able to tell from the change in the migration rate.

Similar to the response rate, it's important to know how long it takes the average prospect to move through each stage of the Loyalty Ladder. That's why you need to track the average migration time at each level in the Loyalty Ladder. Each stage will be different. Some may take ten days; some may take ten months. You need to understand this metric at every marketing stage.

Although related, migration rates are different from response rates, and we keep them separate because they have different purposes.

## Customer Lifetime Value (CLV)

Many businesses consider understanding their customer lifetime value (CLV) the "holy grail" of marketing. And although you might not be able to capture all the nuances of different types of clients, estimating the customer lifetime value is a very good starting point.

You will need some information along the way. The first is the average sales price (ASP) for each product you sell. You might assume, if you have only one product, that the ASP will be the price of your product, but it's a little bit more than that because you might have people that buy multiple things together or buy things multiple times. So for every campaign, for every stage at which there's money changing hands, we need to understand what the ASP of that campaign is going to be, so we need to know that actual revenue.

If you've got sales data you can calculate the ASP from it, but if you're just starting out and building a campaign from scratch, you're going to need to estimate this. Every step on your Loyalty Ladder is going to have an ASP associated with it. Some of will be zero because some stages involve no money transfer, but you might have multiple stages that do involve a money exchange. Not every step on the Loyalty Ladder needs to have an ASP, an average sale price.

You're not going to include here the higher-up steps, which reflect up-selling or repeat buying. Right now, we're just talking about the revenue generated by one campaign alone.

## Expected Revenue Levels (ERL)

Another number that you need to understand is an expected revenue level (ERL). This is a more complex idea. What we're trying to capture is how much each prospect is worth to you at their present stage. Let's ask the question: if you have a storefront and somebody walks in the door, before they've bought anything, how much is that person worth to you? What revenue does that Shopper represent? It's not obvious because they may or may not buy; there may be multiple stages before they buy, so we want to calculate what that value is at a particular point in time. The way that we do it is by calculating the ERL from the revenue generated from the campaigns above it.

For example, if we start with a Looker campaign, we look at its ASP, which may be zero, but there may be some money transaction; it depends on your Loyalty Ladder. Then we add up the expected revenue from all the campaigns that preceded it. The expected revenue starts at the top and works its way down, adding down as you go. That will represent an average. Half of your prospects will be worth more than that and half of your prospects will be worth less than that.

Let me give you an example of how to calculate an ERL. Let's say that you charge $50 for a technical analysis, and 50% of the prospects who receive the analysis will buy the follow-on analysis for $200. It's $50, plus $200 further up the chain thing, and it's a 50% chance that they will buy the $200 item, so it's $50 plus $100 = $150 is the ERL. You need to calculate this at every stage until there is no cost above it. The ERL is the ASP for your top level; then, when you move down one step, you have to take the migration rate into consideration and recalculated the ERL as you move down a step.

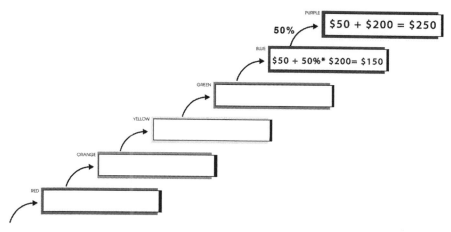

*Figure 6. ERL Calculation*

Let's calculate our expected revenue levels at every level of the following Loyalty Ladder. We've already calculated the migration rate, and we've got those listed on the Loyalty Ladder.

And we have two sales up at the top. There's a "blue" sale and a "purple" sale. So the Customer first buys a product for $50 and then, as a Fan, is up-sold a bigger sale later for $200.

Therefore, the Fan is worth $50 + $200 = $250 while the Customer is worth $50 + 50% * $200 = $150.

Now the good news here is that the value of the Fan is the Customer Lifetime Value. So when we start to calculate the expected revenue at each of these levels, we start at the top.

When we move down a step as in the ERL example we discussed, we're going to combine the ERL of the Customer at the blue level – $150 – with the migration rate.

You can see the buyer ERL is $150 * 25% - the migration rate times the ERL of the step above. That totals $37.50.

We continue the process as we step down the Loyalty Ladder.

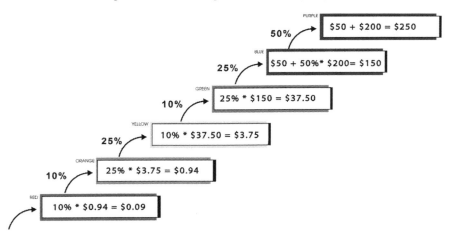

*Figure 7. ERL Calculation*

There's no money associated with the step below, so now we're taking the percentage of the migration and applying it to the ERL above as we step down. For the Shopper, we have $0 plus that 10% of the $37.50 ERL above, or $3.75.

Continue to go down one more step to the Looker and we have 25% of the $3.75 above which is $0.94 or 94 cents.

Step down finally to the Loiterer and we have 10% of $0.94 above which is $0.09 or 9 cents.

What we've done is establish an Expected Revenue Level for each of the groups on the Loyalty Ladder. This tells us how much each of our prospects is worth to us in revenue at each stage. This is an important point that most small business owners do not understand, but it is absolutely critical for you to recognize in order to make intelligent marketing decisions.

For example, if you have a newsletter these migration rates are correct, the calculation above tells you that every newsletter recipient is worth 9 cents. That's a critical piece of information. When they move up to the client education, they're worth 94 cents. When they get a free consultation they're worth $3.75, etc. Now you can decide how much time or effort is worth spending on any prospect at different points in the sales cycle.

These levels may be a little low for this Loyalty Ladder but they tell you what's happening; that's the important part. The reason is because now I can actually tell whether or not this particular marketing plan's going to work. If it costs more than 9 cents or even half of that to get a new person onto my newsletter mailing list, the Loyalty Ladder fails. I have to change how I structure it; I have to change the revenue levels, or I have to change how much I spend to get people in. If I can't do any of these things that tells me this marketing plan is bound to fail.

You can see the importance of understanding these Expected Revenue Levels because they give us a way of quantifying what's happening in our marketing campaigns. It also tells us how much we can spend. There's a lot we do with this as we dig into this information and measure and manage these pieces in-depth so we can see exactly how much we need to spend and exactly where to spend it on these feeder and these marketing campaigns. This is the basis of everything that you need to know to structure a correct campaign.

Okay, so let's talk about measuring those elements. We need to track these ERLs regularly. What elements can we change?

Your average sale price can change, and your migration rates can change. You need to have this chart handy, either in electronic or manual form, and know these numbers because they're very important. If you know how many people are in each pool then you know your expected revenue at any point in time. This is like knowing the value of your prospect database; you can actually put a number on it.

You want to make sure that your spending for each pool is in line. Remember we said if it's forty-seven cents for a newsletter, then you don't want to spend fifty cents getting that person to subscribe to the newsletter. If you do, you're going to run out of money because the migration rates tell you that you won't get enough expected revenue at the end of the process to make it work.

This leads to your return on marketing investment: your estimated revenue for all of your prospects divided by how much you're spending to maintain the Ladder. If, at any point, you know what that revenue is and you know how much you're spending on your marketing campaign to get those people that is your investment; if your return is lower than your investment you're not going to make any money. In fact, you want to get a five- or ten-fold return on that investment; you might want the revenue level of the entire Ladder to be ten or twenty times what you're spending on your marketing campaigns.

These are very important numbers that most small business owners don't understand, but it's critical for you to be able to calculate these things so that you can make an intelligent assessment of how your marketing is performing for you.

Think about your business like a sporting event. You need to keep score. These numbers are your score. You need to communicate these numbers, the potentials and the actuals, to everybody who's involved in sales and marketing. Keep your salespeople in the loop, keep your marketing people in the loop; these critical numbers demonstrate whether you're winning or losing at this game at any particular point in time.

## EXERCISE 13.1 MIGRATION RATES

Estimate the migration rates on your loyalty ladder:

Customer to Fan: _____ (campaign) _____ (rate)

Buyer to Customer: _____ (campaign) _____ (rate)

Shopper to Buyer: _____ (campaign) _____ (rate)

Looker to Shopper: _____ (campaign) _____ (rate)

Loiterer to Looker: _____ (campaign) _____ (rate)

## EXERCISE 13.2 FIND YOUR LIFETIME CUSTOMER VALUE

**Version A. Up-Sell Model**

Typical first purchase: _____

Average Sale Price (ASP) _____ (1)

Typical follow-on purchase: _____

Average Sale Price (ASP) _____ (2)

Percentage of Customers who purchase the follow-on _____ (3)

Lifetime Customer Value (LCV) formula: (1) + (2) * (3) = _____

Note: you can continue this formula if there are more up-selling possibilities by repeating the (2) * (3) component as many times as possible.

**Version B. Repeat Purchase (subscription or usable product)**

Typical first purchase: _____

Average Sale Price (ASP) _____ (1)

Average number of repurchased (or subscription periods, if a subscription _____ (2)

Lifetime Customer Value (LCV) formula: (1) * (2) = _____

Note: you can combine versions A and B together if necessary.

# Chapter 14. The Platform

## What is a Marketing Platform?

A marketing platform is like your soapbox. It's the position you can stand on in order to reach more people, to cast your voice into a wider audience. It literally is just like a platform: the higher and the wider it is, the taller you can stand and the further your voice will extend. All of the work we've done so far in far in solidifying your market in order to scale your business has referred to creating the messaging for a solid and growing business. Now, you need the platform in order to cast your voice as widely and as loudly as possible.

There's a number of different ways to do that but most companies scale best when they're able to add additional channels to their platform, enlarge in the group of people they're talking to (the "tribe," to use Seth Godin's term), and broaden the niche that they're focusing on so that they have a larger group of people who are eligible to hear their voice.

When you think about channels, you should think about it just like you would on a television or a radio. There are different ways that people can tune in to hear what you have to say; the more ways that you're able to be found, the more modes through which you're communicating, the better off you'll be.

It's important to think about moving beyond the channels that you have today. Examples of channels are blogging, newsletters, video, podcast, and television. These are all different ways that you could be communicating with your audience. Take some time to do an inventory of the channels you use today. Think about which ones that you use on a regular basis and feel like you have some competency in. You want to look at how you might broaden those channels in different ways.

Enlarging your tribe is about continually focusing on getting more and more people to hear your voice. This is a little bit different than marketing. It's true that it should be our goal to get more customers, but in tribe building, the main objective is actually to get more people to listen, to pay attention to you on a regular basis, whether or not they purchase from you.

Scaling your company and your platform is about having listeners, not Buyers. That's not to say that you shouldn't be concerned about monetizing your platform but we've already discussed how to take eyeballs and turn them into revenue. But in some sense you still have to solve the problem of getting more eyeballs. This comes down to a focus on enlarging your audience continuously.

Your marketing efforts should be directed at getting more and more people to opt in and to join our community, whether or not they provide us with an e-mail address. You want to make sure that there's a way for them to join, and your objective should be to get them to join. Sometimes this is just a shift in mindset from trying to find a customer or only being interested in marketing to customers versus trying to build a following. A following may consist of people who are not just potential customers but are also people who do things that similar to what you do.

This is okay. A lot of people are afraid that if they attract a following, it may consist of potentially competitors, and that might endanger our future revenue. You can't think like this. It's important that you think about reaching out to more and more people as an element of abundance: the more you give, the more you get back. These people maybe competitors but they may also be sources of referrals.

Finally, enlarging or broadening your niche is the third way of expanding your reach. We talked a little bit about doing that when we talked about monetizing what we do in a different way. Think about where you provide services and whether or not you can provide ancillary services before or after you engage a Customer, or offer something related to what you do currently. This is also a way to think about expanding from your current target market into adjacent target markets that would be similar in products and services that you offer today.

## Add Channels

Let's talk for a minute about the channels that are available to broaden your reach. The first channel that many small business owners use is blogging. It used to be said that every small business owner had to have a blog. I don't believe that's necessarily true, but a blog is a powerful way of getting your voice out there. If you don't currently have a blog, you should think about whether it makes sense for you. Creating a blog is easier than it used to be, but keeping it fresh and popular is much more difficult. With new tools such as WordPress, it's easy to create a professional looking blog with a design that is tasteful and professional.

If you want to get started quickly, install a copy of WordPress on your host server and purchase a theme or download a free one that is consistent with your brand. If you aren't good at configuring these sorts of things, it makes sense to get a professional to help. You don't want a blog that looks like it's been put together by a twelve-year-old. If you decide to blog, commit to doing so on a regular basis. "Regular basis" means posting new content at least weekly. Anything less often shows that you're not really committed to producing new content; people won't visit your blog or subscribe to your updates, which makes your efforts futile.

There are other ways of getting your content out in writing without having a blog. You can post updates to other platforms, such as LinkedIn or Facebook or other people's blogs. Guest posting on other blogs is a great way to get started in building an audience. It should be a part of your repertoire if you choose to write, but you may run into the problem if the audience you're building remains someplace else. One of the good arguments for having your own blog is that audience and the traffic comes to you, and once they're on your site, you can talk to them in any way that makes the most sense. You're much more restricted when you use another person's platform. It's what Nicholas Carr[2] called "digital sharecropping," and it means you're building your business on someone else's land.

Another channel available to you is writing a book. This may seem like a formidable task, and many people who want to write books find that they can't muster the energy to do so. With the tools available today, it's much easier to write a book than it has ever been.

There are two types of books that you should consider: an e-book or a published, printed book. In general, the only difference between an e-book and a printed book is length. It's been thought that e-books are of slightly lower quality than printed books, but I think the only difference should be length; the quality should be the same. You don't want your e-book to be seen as sub-par. It should be of a quality which, if it were just a little bit longer and made sense from a cost perspective, could be printed on paper and bound.

If you're thinking of creating an e-book, there are a number of ways to go about it. An e-book can be created very quickly, sometimes in as little as a weekend. It's all about finding the right theme, sitting down, and either writing or transcribing content, having it edited, getting a nice cover for it, and publishing either on your own website or on another distribution site, such as Amazon. If you're struggling to

---

[2] http://www.roughtype.com/?p=634

figure out a way to do this, there are people who specialize in helping small business owners get e-books published. Finding some good resources on Elance is a good place to get started. If you decide to publish your book in a printed format, the fundamental question becomes whether or not you should self-publish or spend the time to go to a traditional publishing house.

Several years ago, self-published books were seen as inferior to books that were published by traditional publishing houses. I believe this is no longer the case. It depends on your purpose in publishing your book. If you're trying to create an audience and have some authority to widen your marketing platform, it's not necessary to go to a traditional publisher.

It's true that some more experienced authors can benefit from the marketing power of large publishing houses, but that happens so infrequently it's not worth pursuing as an income source. It's more important to publish your material and get it out into the world so that you can build a marketing platform from it, have control over its distribution and how it's used. The moment you go to a traditional publisher, you lose some of those choices and you'll be required to submit to the publishing guidelines of the traditional publishing house.

Another potential channel is the use of audio or video. Audio and video is used primarily for one of two purposes: to train or entertain. Either way, it builds a channel for you to get your message out. If you choose to train, you'll need to develop a course or a set of small lessons that you can turn into audio or video. Publishing these on a number of different platforms – your website, other training platform websites, or YouTube – is up to you, but make sure that you direct traffic to it in a way that captures the contact information of your audience. This is much more difficult if you use another platform, such as YouTube, or a training platform. On the other hand, those platforms are able to direct traffic that your website may not capture.

Another, not-often-thought-of opportunity with audio and video is to use it for entertainment. This is typically not done alone, and depends primarily on the type of business that you have, but it is an opportunity to create interaction with what you do by capturing people's attention for a brief moment and going viral – getting people to come back over and over again to see something entertaining. If you choose to go in this direction, make sure that this an area where you have either some skill or expert support to help you develop an appropriate entertainment vehicle. It's not easy to create something that can be consumed by the public as entertainment. There are formulas that work and things that don't work. Don't try to learn all of these things by making the mistakes yourself. Get professional assistance.

Another channel that might be available to you is podcasting. Podcasting is becoming a very successful and popular endeavor, but is still used much less frequently than some other vehicles, such as blogging. Once you have a successful podcast, you can tap into an audience that comes back on a regular basis to listen to what you have to say.

There are two typical formats of podcasts: topic-based or interview-based. If you pursue the topic-based broadcast, your ability to establish your authority is primarily based on what you know about a given topic. Some new podcasters are trying a hybrid model of both since it can be difficult to consistently locate quality interview subjects.

My first podcast, *Scale to Success*, is a hybrid model in which we interview a new business owner every few weeks; in between, we provide our own content according to the Four Keys of Scale that we've been discussing in this book.

There are great resources to learn how to podcast. I'll turn your attention to probably one of the best that I'm familiar with, which is John Lee Dumas' freepodcastcourse.com, available online. John Lee Dumas is the creator of the very popular *Entrepreneur on Fire* podcast, and has shared his secrets about how to create a podcast with his audience.

Another option is using webinars or web broadcasting. A webinar is a half-hour or one-hour web broadcast through which you teach an audience something that you know. Sometimes people use webinars to sell a product; sometimes they simply use it to educate and provide value to their audience.

A web broadcast is a "live," interactive or broadcast show that doesn't necessarily have a structured script, but features the more the natural interaction style of the host, either with the audience or with other co-hosts. Either way, this can be used much like audio and video – that is, for training or as entertainment. Webinars are becoming are becoming a very popular platforms for build audiences.

Another very powerful platform is public speaking. Going out and getting public speaking engagements is a terrific way to build a following. Standing on stage and delivering content to a live audience, though, can be quite frightening for people who are not comfortable with public speaking, so this is not for everyone. If you enjoy being in front of an audience, capturing an audience's attention, and are capable of holding that attention for a period of time, this could be a very powerful way for you to expand your audience.

Getting paid for a speaking engagement, however, can be very difficult. Often, there are many people who want to speak in order get in front of an audience and, therefore, are willing to do it for free. You need to make a decision about whether or not that fits your marketing plan. For example, if you are trying to get in front of an audience and capture their contact information in order to communicate with them or sell them product later, it may make sense to ahead and speak for free, assuming that your target market is in the audience.

If you're trying to expand your income by becoming a keynote speaker or getting paid to run workshops, that is a different business model. Generally, to get these kinds of engagements you need to establish your credibility and build an audience over time in order to have a following. You'll need to assemble a speaker's kit that is available for meeting planners to review your past work. Make sure as you do free speaking engagements to capture testimonials, and capture yourself on video, so that as your speaking engagements grow, you can add these clips to your speaker's kit. Many speakers have found that once they decide it's time to get paid to speak that they don't have any video footage of their past speeches; they have to create something from scratch in order to develop the marketing materials they need.

The last channel that I want to discuss is television broadcasting. By television, I don't necessarily mean cable or satellite. There are a number of digital media sources that are delivered either via broadcast TV or cable, but they can also be delivered via Internet. The idea here is to create an entertaining program. This is an expensive channel, but can be very powerful if done correctly. Much like audio and video as entertainment vehicles, you will need a professional to assist you. If you can capture an appropriate message from your business in a television show, whether as an entertainment vehicle or as a reality/educational TV show, you can significantly expand the reach of your audience by providing content in a way that is very rare to your audience.

No matter which channels you choose, you should go through an inventory of the ones you use today and decide which ones you would like to expand into in the future. You should expand slowly over time, but certainly should pick the channels that you might be interested in and put them on a list so that you can strategize how you use the information in a different way and what information or resources (such as video footage) you need to collect. Also, as we've discussed before, it's important to think about expanding into these channels by leveraging your existing content. If you want to move into audio and video, there are ways of doing that by leveraging your blog or existing written materials. Likewise, many people have published their first book by simply pulling together a bunch of their blog posts. There's nothing wrong with this, as people typically will consume your content in different channels; they expect to see consistency across your content. They do not consider the fact that they've seen the material before as repetition, but simply as brand consistency. What you might think of as a negative actually turns into a positive.

## Enlarge Your Tribe

Growing your tribe is about capturing a larger audience in the channels that you've selected. As I've pointed out before, the biggest challenge is a change in mindset, the fact that attracting an audience is primarily about gaining a following rather than selling something. You'll have an opportunity to sell to that audience later, but the first thing you want to do is have an audience who's paying attention to what you have to sell.

Very similar to the Loyalty Ladder that we created earlier, you want to think about feeding that Loyalty Ladder with a bigger and bigger audience. If you don't own an audience, you'll have to purchase an audience someplace else. It's a very expensive way to acquire new prospects. But if you have an audience and it belongs to you, then there are a number of things you can do with it. Not only is it much less expensive to acquire new prospects for your products, but you can actually survey that audience and find out what they want to in order to help you identify new and different ways to diversify your income.

It's often said that the money is in the "list," so you need to do whatever you can to build your "list." That means leveraging channels and capturing information at every possible opportunity. Provide value through your channels so that you have an excuse to ask people for their e-mail addresses. Make sure you have an e-mail database to capture this information, and communicate with your audience on a regular basis. That communication needs to be value-added. You need to be able to provide value about eighty percent of the time, and use only twenty percent of the time to talk about you and the products that you offer or sell.

As you continue to add value over time and communicate with this tribe through more and more channels, you'll find that the tribe actually becomes quite loyal to you. Certainly, there will be people who will drop out over time because they opt out of whatever it is that you have to offer, but it's the loyalty of the ones who remain that you want to engender.

Be personable with this group. Be magnanimous. If you are seen as a good human being who gives, there will be a great deal of loyalty directed to you from the people who listen to you on a regular basis.

It takes time to build a tribe, so the number one thing to remember is patience. You're going to have to expend some effort in over an extended period of time to build a tribe. It would be surprising if you were able to build a significant tribe in anything less than a six-month period of time, so expect to spend months building your tribe before monetizing it. If that means that you need to have other income sources available during that time, don't shut off your existing products or services until that tribe is available. It may be work that you have to do in parallel. This may require extra effort on your part, but it'll be worth it as you develop a loyal following that is waiting for your next product.

## Broaden Niche

Finally, a solid marketing platform is built upon a broad niche of services. As I've discussed before, it's important to think about the products and services you offer and how they fit into the daily life of your prospect or Customer. Think about things that you can offer either before or after your engagement in your current product or service, or adjacent markets that you can access. Can you provide support for the product or service that you create? What happens, typically, when your customer no longer needs your product or service; what do they need next or instead? Can you provide the next step or the upgrade to it? It's important that you think about the niche that you fill, that you always look for opportunities to expand. Pushing into those expansion areas is a strategic decision. It should be timed appropriately because it's important to remain focused during a growth period. As you scale, you'll want to pick additional areas, one by one, and focus on them, as well.

Don't cast too wide a net all at once or your efforts will be diluted across a number of different areas. Think of it as a brand new start-up within your existing company. In some sense it needs to be treated like that. You'll need to go back and do the same things you did to create your original company, and create new processes as you learn in a new area: that means creating a Minimum Viable Product, serving customers, getting feedback and solidifying your offering in a new area. This work is worth it as you are able to create a broader base of income that diversifies what you do and gives you the opportunity to tap into markets that you're currently not in.

## EXERCISE 14.1 THE PLATFORM

1. Do an inventory of the channels you use today. How many of these channels are you current active in?

Blog _____

E-book _____

Printed book _____

Audio training _____

Video training _____

Podcast _____

Webinars _____

Web broadcasts _____

Public speaking _____

Video broadcast (TV) _____

2. Going through that same list, how many of these channels *should* you be active in? Make this a wish list. Don't focus on how you'll do it yet.

Blog _____

E-book _____

Printed book _____

Audio training _____

Video training _____

Podcast _____

Webinars _____

Web broadcasts _____

Public speaking _____

Video broadcast (TV) _____


3. For the channels you currently aren't using, how will you find an expert or team to get you into those channels? What sources will you use? _____

_____

_____

4. Where will you need to change your opt-in messaging to focus on gathering an audience rather than on selling a product? _____

_____

_____

5. What other niches or target markets can you access which will broaden your base of potential customers? _____

_____

_____

# Section 5. The Processes

# Chapter 15. Marketing Automation

## Lead Generation

The number one task you need to take care of in order to scale your business is automating your marketing functions. You can't automate a marketing function without automated lead generation. Typically in servicing companies in which the sole owner is responsible for all sales and marketing, lead generation is done by an individual who manually looks up potential prospects, or leverages referrals or people they already know from their Rolodex. When you have a small client base, and that's the only thing you need to keep your business going, this is a perfectly fine thing to do. But as you grow your company and need to move beyond your own personal resources, you will have to develop another way to generate leads.

There are a number of ways to go about automating lead generation, but the first is defining a process by which you're going to get new leads. That may be through understanding the client profiles you developed in the beginning. Those client profiles will give you a sense of who you need to be talking to, and what messages will resonate with them. You then need to figure out where these people can be found so you can deploy automated lead capture in these areas.

If you find that your target market is hanging out online, you can use lead magnets to capture e-mail addresses of these prospects and communicate with them directly. If you find that the best place to find your target customers is at marketing events, such as trade shows, then you'll need to engage in a marketing effort that will put you in front of those people at trade shows. In some cases, the leads you need to generate are people who are neither online giving their e-mail address away, nor at public events. For example, if you are trying to target CEOs of companies, you may need to do that through a direct mail outreach.

It's often thought that direct marketing is no longer effective. That's not true. Direct marketing can still be very effective if it's done correctly. The major problem with most direct marketing efforts is that it's not consistent and easily ignored, and it doesn't build trust with your prospect. You need to develop trust with your audience just as you would if you were operating an e-mail campaign, just substituting an e-mail address with a lead magnet. You should think about your lead generation activities as a process – essentially an autoresponder of some kind – whether it's an e-mail autoresponder, or a mail autoresponder, or a direct phone call; there needs to be a campaign with clear messages assigned to different need segments with different triggers.

Imagine you were going to set up your lead generation process in some kind of campaign management software like Infusionsoft. Even if it's not an e-mail, the process should be as well-defined. Take some time to map out a lead generation process that will get you in front of the right people and build trust with them over time. Think about the elements that will establish credibility for you and that will help you build a relationship so that when it comes time to have a sales conversation, the appropriate person can do that because the organization has built up loyalty.

Once you've defined that process, map that process against the appropriate resources and/or people that you need to execute that process. Not all processes need to be performed by computers. The important thing here is that you have a process that is defined and well understood, and that you could bring in a human being to execute that process, if necessary, with the appropriate training. Sometimes, lead generation is best done by people who can dynamically have a conversation and build relationships. If that's the case, it's fine as long as you define exactly where that step of the process belongs. As we've discussed in previous chapters, there's a role for human beings in the sales process, versus a longer-term relationship building and marketing process, but lead generation is the idea of collecting a qualified prospect's name and address or e-mail and starting the process.

You can't do this unless you understand your qualification guidelines. Write down the descriptive elements of your customer profile that would fit your qualifications for having a conversation. Make sure that this is well-understood by everyone throughout the organization so you're not spending time chasing down leads that would be a waste of time. Once you have qualifications, a defined process, and then a map to the resources or people who will execute that process, you have a scalable lead generation framework that you can automate.

## Prospect Communication

At some point, after the lead has been generated, you have a prospect with whom you need to be able to communicate. In order to clarify the different types of communication, I'm going to break this down into e-mail and non-e-mail communications. E-mail communication is probably one of the most important functions of a scalable sales and marketing process. It's very rare that a company can scale without electronic communication.

The good news is that most communication is the same, regardless of its format. So whether you e-mail, direct mail or call, the messages are basically the same. If you think about communication as breaking down into four major categories, divided out by the dimensions of relationship-building versus sales, and manual e-mails versus automated ones, you can classify how you should communicate with your prospects.

This fits into a four-box diagram in which the first type of e-mail communication is called "networking." These are manual relationship-building e-mails that you would send out to start a conversation. This can't be automated; this can't be a mass e-mail because significant personalization is required in order to understand the needs of that person and to build a network with them.

The second type is called "direct outreach." These are manual, sales-oriented e-mails. Direct outreach e-mails are intended to introduce yourself and to create a potential Value Proposition with the prospect. This also needs to be done manually because, typically, these people have not opted-in to receive automated communication from you. In addition, because you're trying to build credibility and loyalty, you need to be able to outline a Value Proposition that makes sense to them.

The third kind is called "Care and Feeding." These are automated relationship-building e-mails. Typically, "Care and Feeding" e-mails are used when the prospect is not yet ready to buy; there will be a longer sales cycle during which you need to build trust and credibility over time. A "Care and Feeding" campaign typically educates and adds value to the prospect over a longer period of time so that you can eventually have a sales conversation.

The fourth kind is called the "qualified offer." These are automated sales-oriented e-mails. "Qualified offers" are opportunities for you to go out with a service offering to your prospect once it is clear that they have qualified themselves through some kind of trigger. Because this is pre-qualified, it can't be considered automated.

The only difference in communication between B2B versus those that sell B2C is in the price point of the solution. Companies that sell low-priced consumer (and some business) goods will likely not spend much time personalizing communication; it just doesn't make much sense for them in the long-run.

On the other hand, expensive consumer goods and services can often feel like commercial opportunities. Here it makes some sense to make each manually sent message feel unique.

## Customer Service

The automated portion of your customer service should involve two major parts: one, automating your outreach to the customer to help them use the product or service you've just sold them, and two, occasionally surveying them to make sure that they're satisfied. These two things are not difficult to do, though they're generally overlooked or can be done inappropriately.

In order to automate the outreach to your customer after they've purchased, define a process whereby you have several, regular points of contact with the customer after they purchase. These can be defined around milestones that are natural to your product or service, such as the first time they use it or the first month of renewal, but they could be just general outreach points, such as every month or so. It's a "best practice" to communicate more often at the beginning of the relationship and leave more time between points of contact as the relationship continues. For example, you might find it helpful to contact the customer after the first month of using your product and then every month for the first six months, but then scale back to six months to a year between contacts after a few years have gone by.

It's also a good idea to reach out when there are specific things that are about to happen, such as a renewal, or in the expiration of a warranty or a guarantee, to make sure that you are proactive in resolving any concerns that might exist. Surveying the customer is a very important part of your marketing plan. Remember that the goal of your marketing plan is to generate additional sales and more leads, and there is no better place to find those than from satisfied Customer who become Fans. And there is no way to know if a Customer is satisfied unless you ask them.

Surveying can be fraught with peril. You have to be careful not to over survey or to survey on every interaction. There are a number of companies that survey after every interaction in order to collect data. This causes two major problems: one, survey fatigue when people are no longer interested in participating in the survey because they are asked every single time, and two, you do not get accurate data from your surveys because the only participants are ones who have something negative to say (this is more insidious and just as inaccurate). That typically gives you the wrong impression of what's happening with your Customer.

It's better to define a regular time period for surveys to go out, or after major interactions, and keep the survey short and to the point. You shouldn't have to collect demographics from your customer because you should already have them as part of your Customer data.

Lots of people like to use anonymous surveys to collect market research data. This is a great idea if you're surveying people you don't know, but if you're sending a survey to one of your Customers, it should absolutely be connected to their customer record so if there is a problem you can do something about it. That means you can skip a whole bunch of questions on demographics and psychographics unless you believe that something has changed dramatically since they purchased your product or service.

If there are major touch points, such as a service complaint that needs to be resolved, or a major event in the life of your product, such as a renewal, then you might want to survey in advance of those times. For example, if you have a renewal coming up at the end of the year, it's important to get information about how satisfied the Customer is before the renewal event occurs, not afterwards when they choose not to renew.

Asking a Customer why they didn't renew is too late. They can give you great feedback, but you generally can't save the sale in these cases. If, however, you inform the customer in advance that a renewal is coming up and address any concerns before they have to make the decision, you might be able to salvage a sale that otherwise would be lost from a client who would leave.

It's important to remember that the goal of these surveys is to automate them as much as possible, however, there are times where surveying should not be done in an automated fashion. For example, after a major service complaint, somebody should personally talk to the Customer and make sure that they are satisfied. This should not be an automated survey to rate how we did, on a scale of 1 - 5. This should be a conversation whose notes are captured in a customer record in your CRM that someone reviews.

Done well, automated communication with your Customer to understand how they're using your product or service and how satisfied they are can ensure that more Customers become Fans and eventually sources of referrals, leads, and potentially more revenue.

## Up-Selling, Cross-Selling, and Referrals

The final step of any marketing campaign should be ensuring that you have additional revenue opportunities through up-selling and cross-selling existing Customers. This can be automated by segmenting customers into the product segments that they would most likely be eligible to join. This means that you should know, based on the behavior of your customers, how they use their product, and how they interact with you, what they would most-likely buy next. If you don't have anything else for them to buy, there may be an opportunity to continue renewing the product they're using today, and look for new product opportunities in the future.

Either way, it's important for you to establish a regular time frame that you'll reach out to existing Customers and give them the opportunity to deepen their financial engagement with you. This works best when it is preceded by a customer satisfaction survey that ensures there are no outstanding problems. Believe it or not, Customers who have service failures that are resolved satisfactorily are actually *more* likely to purchase an additional product because of the experience of having their problem resolved.

Therefore, it's critical to align customer satisfaction and problem resolution with an opportunity to cross-sell and up-sell. Clearly, there are going to be times where this isn't the right approach and your judgment should prevail, but the goal is to have an automated process in place in which customer life cycle events are triggered for you to be able to cross-sell and up-sell.

As you become larger, you're able to use customer data in order to improve the relevancy of your offers. In the meantime, it's important to collect as much data as possible to understand your Customers, the types of products they buy, and how they use the products. Use that information to help you understand better what product they might purchase next. This type of information is critical to being able not only to automate but optimize the process of cross-selling and up-selling.

## EXERCISE 15.1 MARKETING AUTOMATION - LEAD GENERATION

1. Develop a list of pre-qualification questions that identify an ideal lead. These questions should include both demographic and behavioral qualifications. Have at least 5.

    1. _____

    2. _____

    3. _____

    4. _____

    5. _____

2. Identify at least 3 different sources for leads. Avoid generic sources such as "the internet."

    1. _____

    2. _____

    3. _____

3. Define a process by which leads are sourced and pre-qualification questions are assessed. Diagram the process like a flowchart.

4. Assign each step of the process onto a person or resource (human or technology) that will execute that step. _____

_____

_____

_____

## EXERCISE 15.2 MARKETING AUTOMATION - PROSPECT COMMUNICATION

The use of e-mail

For each of the four major e-mail classifications identify:

A. Is it relevant to your marketing process?

B. For manual processes, who will be responsible for sending?

C. For automated processes, what tool will you use for sending?

D. For automated processes, who will be responsible for writing?

"Care and Feeding" E-mails (Automated and Relationship-Building)

Relevant? _____

What tool will send these e-mails? _____

Who will write the e-mails? _____

Qualified Call-to-Action E-mails (Automated and Sales-Oriented)

Relevant? _____

What tool will send these e-mails? _____

Who will write the e-mails? _____

Networking E-mails (Manual and Relationship-Building)

Relevant? (Yes)

Who will be responsible for writing and sending? _____

Direct Outreach E-mails (Manual and Sales-Oriented)

Relevant? (Yes)

Who will be responsible for writing and sending? _____

## EXERCISE 15.3 MARKETING AUTOMATION - CUSTOMER SERVICE

Part I. Customer Service and Support

1. Identify the service triggers that will generate an outbound message from your organization? (For example, renewal, warranty expiration, major usage spikes, etc.)

_____

_____

2. Align each service trigger with the message you wish to send:

Trigger Message

_____    _____

_____    _____

_____    _____

_____    _____

Part II. Customer Satisfaction

1. Identify the time frame and/or events that will generate an outbound customer satisfaction survey. Do not over survey.

_____

_____

2. What five (no more than 5) questions will you ask?

_____

_____

_____

_____

# EXERCISE 15.4 MARKETING AUTOMATION - UP-SELLING, CROSS-SELLING, AND REFERRALS

1. Identify the trigger events where your customer is happy and receiving the perceived benefit? (Note: after a positive customer satisfaction survey should be one of the options.)

_____

_____

_____

_____

2. Identify customer segments that might be interested in different follow-on products. Indicate how you will differentiate the customer segment (if it isn't obvious) and which product will be the next most likely.

Segment Identification Next Product

| | | |
|---|---|---|
| _____ | _____ | _____ |
| _____ | _____ | _____ |
| _____ | _____ | _____ |
| _____ | _____ | _____ |
| _____ | _____ | _____ |

3. What are your referral incentives?

_____

_____

_____

# Chapter 16. Sales Execution

## The Role of Sales in Marketing

One of the most difficult areas in marketing is getting the sales and the marketing groups to cooperate with each other. Often, companies that I work with have a difficult time figuring out where the role of marketing ends and the role of sales begins, and vice versa.

The challenge is that sales thinks that anything that has to do with the prospect is their domain, but it's just not efficient to have the sales department work with every single prospect. There are certainly going to be prospects for whom human interaction with a salesperson will be more effective than anything else you do, but that's not the case in every situation.

I like to distinguish the roles of marketing and sales in the following way: marketing is the entire campaign process that we've put together using the Loyalty Ladder, and gaining the trust and credibility of the prospect over time; sales is the specific effort of having a human being work with a prospect. It could very well be that a prospect can close themselves and not require interaction with a salesperson at all, but there will be cases in which human interaction is required for your prospect to determine if they want to buy your product or service.

In those cases, we need to determine where in the Loyalty Ladder the sales function actually belongs so that we can overlay the sales process and the marketing process.

In general, a salesperson is going to have a difficult time engaging effectively with someone who has not at least moved to the Shopper phase. Just a quick reminder, a Shopper is a prospect that has an identified a need and is now interested in facts and figures to solve their problem.

Human beings do a very good job of listening to people's needs, hearing the unspoken desires of the prospect, and translating those desires into the benefits of the product or service they're offering. That's generally not the best use of an automated function, although it certainly can be the case if you have a product or service that scales quite nicely.

On the flip side, human beings are an expensive resource to use for educating people about what you do, or trying to paint a vision to encourage your prospect to develop the need for your product or service. These are things that are best handled by automation.

There will be always exceptions to these rules, but you should think very carefully about having people spend a lot of time focused on prospects that have not, at least, identified a need for the product or service you sell.

In some cases, such as where the product or service is new or unique or fills a need that many people don't believe they have, you may need salespeople to engage earlier in the Loyalty Ladder, beginning at the Looker phase, so that they can help the prospect develop the need over time. Often, these salespeople are called "evangelists" because their real role is to help people understand why they would have the need for what you're selling.

Evangelists spend time creating a vision and painting a picture of what a prospect's life would be like after having their problem solved. Since the problem is one that the prospect may not even recognize they have, it's important that a human being be engaged to help develop this need. Generally speaking, it's important to know that you need to have a separation between when a human being gets involved and when marketing plays its role. That means that your organization should have a very specific plan for handing off a lead to sales, and for sales handing the lead back to marketing.

In this chapter we're going to talk about where sales belongs in the Loyalty Ladder. We're going to talk about what sales needs to do differently in order to engage with marketing, and what should happen if sales needs to hand off a Prospect back to marketing.

## Where Sales Belongs in the Loyalty Ladder

Let's get very specific here and think about the Loyalty Ladder that you've developed earlier in the book. We're going to look at each stage to determine whether or not this is something that a salesperson should handle. Take a look at each stage from Loiterer to Looker to Shopper to Buyer, and determine whether or not a human being is required to deliver on the Value Proposition that you've defined.

It's important that you think about the most efficient and effective way of delivering the Value Proposition. Generally speaking, salespeople are best engaged at the Shopper and Buyer stages, and are usually not effective in the Looker and Loiterer stages. However, that could change if you target market is such that your prospect doesn't understand the problem you're trying to solve, or if the One Big Result you're trying to achieve is something that is not easily understood.

In addition to having direct sales, there should be an automated approach to delivering on the Value Proposition, as well. For each stage of your Loyalty Ladder, you should identify whether or not a salesperson is involved and how you can deliver on the Value Proposition.

Here are the questions that you should ask yourself:

What would the salesperson do to deliver the Value Proposition?

Is a human being required to deliver the value that we promise in this stage?

Is there a more efficient way of delivering that Value Proposition?

As you answer these questions for each step of the Loyalty Ladder, you can understand where to best deploy your sales force. Keep in mind that there are different roles in the sales process that often will correspond to different stages on the Loyalty Ladder.

The classic consultative salesperson is often best deployed in the Shopper phase, while a technical sales or demo sales resource is often best deployed in evangelist scenarios in the Looker phase.

A quick note about demos: companies that have software or a product that can be demonstrated can use it as a powerful part of the sales process, but it's important to know the purpose of giving the demo, and the goal of the exercise. There are two categories of demonstrations: ones that occur at the Looker phase, and ones that occur at the Shopper phase. These are two very different demonstrations with very different purposes, and should not be confused.

If you're doing demos and don't have two very different styles of demonstration, you're not talking to the right audience at the right time. The Looker demo should be focused on creating a picture of what a day in the prospect's life would be with the use of your product. You should focus on workflow, on daily tasks, and not on features and additions to the product that don't come into play on a day-to-day basis. You want to tell stories about typical use cases and describe how life would be better or easier or cheaper using your product or service.

When you move to a demo at the Shopper phase your prospect has already identified that they are in the market for what you have to sell, so you don't have to convince them that their life would be better. What you have to do is convince them that your product can deliver on the promise of the better life that you sold them in the earlier Looker stage.

This demo should focus on benefits that specifically differentiate your product from others that may be in consideration. This is where you can spend some time focusing on those special items in the menu or the individual features that allow your user to accomplish something that they wouldn't otherwise be able to accomplish.

This is a very different type of demonstration. It's typically longer, with much more Q&A. It's much more interactive. It's important that of the Shopper demonstration focus on answering the question: why choose us? The Looker demo should focus on answering the question: what is in it for me? These are two very different demonstrations. Companies often make the mistake of not differentiating their demo based on where the prospect is in the sales cycle. This is a mistake that often comes up later when demos have to be performed again, or when there is difficulty in getting the prospect to move to a more in-depth conversation about your product.

## Learning to Close to the Next Step

One of the biggest challenges salespeople face when integrating with a comprehensive marketing system is learning their role at every stage of the process. Most salespeople are programmed to "close the deal," however, in an integrated marketing campaign where the goal is simply to move a prospect from one stage to the next, it's important that salespeople understand that their job is to close to the next step.

For example, if in your Loyalty Ladder you have a salesperson engaged in an introductory conversation in order to suggest that the prospect engage in a needs assessment, the salesperson needs to understand that the entire focus of their conversation should be dedicated to getting the needs assessment done and not to try to understand all of the purchasing elements necessary to get a contract signed.

Many times salespeople think they understand this point but have a difficult time sticking with the goal "in the moment" because they're so excited about a sales opportunity and want to close it as quickly as possible. This is even more so in cases where sales may engage in one part of the Loyalty Ladder simply to turn it back over to an automated process later. This may seem counterintuitive but there are times when this is the right thing to do. For example, in cases in which salespeople spend a great deal of time evangelizing about their product or service, they may decide to have a human being focused on building need, but then turn the prospect over to an automated needs assessment in order to qualify them and do product selection.

This might seem like taking a step backwards, but as long as the automated process is focused on continuing to develop the need for the prospect and contact is being maintained, this may be a very efficient way of moving the prospect through what could otherwise be a very labor-intensive process.

Each person at each stage of the process needs to understand their role and what they're trying to accomplish. Therefore, communicating the stage of the marketing campaign and having everyone understand the full impact of the Loyalty Ladder is critical to success.

## Moving from Sales Back to "Care and Feeding"

When is it time to turn our prospect back over to the automated marketing and away from a live salesperson? This is a difficult question for a lot of organizations, and many salespeople are hesitant about doing this, but a scalable organization understands when a prospect no longer qualifies to be handled by a live salesperson. In most cases, the reason the salesperson does not want to admit that their prospect is not going to convert comes down to one of two reasons: 1. they're having trouble figuring out how they're going to meet their sales quotas, or 2. they don't trust that if they let the prospect go, the prospect will be handled appropriately.

The first is an individual issue associated with the salesperson. Salespeople need to understand that they won't be able to hit their sales quotas with unqualified prospects, and they should spend their time looking for ones that will drive them toward their goal. This is a little bit of a mental block for most salespeople because they feel that if they've invested a lot of time with the person, they're close to closing, but this is not often the case when a prospect has stopped making progress. After a prospect has stopped making progress, they're more likely to remain stagnant or move back down the Loyalty Ladder than they are to close the deal. A salesperson's time is better spent investing with those prospects that are making active progress.

The second problem is one of communication and process. It should be your responsibility, as the business owner, to develop the processes that ensure that the salespeople's prospects will be handled appropriately when they are handed back to marketing. A proper handoff involves explaining to the prospect what's happening and continuing to provide value along the way.

Generally, the prospect, if they're not making forward progress, doesn't object to this handoff. In some cases, the process itself encourages the prospect to move along on their own because they feel that they'll either stop getting value or stop having contact with the salesperson who has been helping them solve the particular business problem. In either case, it's important to have a "Care and Feeding" campaign as part of your marketing automation.

This "Care and Feeding" campaign can take many forms. It can be an e-mail campaign; it can be video tutorials; it can be a newsletter; it could be quarterly phone calls, but it should be a regular form of communication that continues to add value.

The communication should be completely automated and not require human assistance on a prospect-by-prospect basis until the prospect becomes qualified again. Every single piece of communication that goes out through your "Care and Feeding" campaign should include a call-to-action where prospects can self-select back into the sales process. This call-to-action typically encourages Shoppers to start thinking through the positives and negatives of the product or service that's being offered. No communication should go out to a prospect that doesn't include a call-to-action of some kind, even if that call-to-action is simply "hit reply" and answer a question.

Surveys are great ways to keep prospects in a "Care and Feeding" campaign engaged. The only recommendation is to not over-survey. It's important that prospects not feel that communicating with a company they don't plan to buy from will take up too much of their time, but regular communication is important. Irregular communication, or only sending out something when you have something to sell, gives the wrong impression to the prospect. That regular value-add is important.

Keep in mind all communication should fit the eighty-twenty rule: eighty percent of your communication should add value to your prospect by sharing information, while twenty percent can be spent in discussing sales offers or other interesting things about the company — which of course, should also add value. Each of these cases provides an opportunity for the sales team to execute their job in a way that is most effective and supportive of the automation that's occurring. When that's done, the metrics can be measured, which allow you as a business owner to manage the effectiveness of your sales team.

## EXERCISE 16.1 SALES EXECUTION

1. Where in the Loyalty Ladder will a live salesperson get involved?

_____

2. What signal or behavioral trigger will you be looking for to see if sales should get involved?

_____

3. What kind of training will have to occur to keep the sales staff focused on "closing to the next step of the Loyalty Ladder" rather than "closing the sale?"

_____

4. How will you know when it's time for your prospect to leave the live sales funnel and move back into a "Care and Feeding" campaign?

_____

5. What will your "Care and Feeding" campaign look like?

_____

A. What value will you add? _____

B. How often will you communicate? _____

C. How will you know it's time for the prospect to re-engage in the sales process? _____

D. What call-to-action will you offer to elicit that trigger?

_____

_____

# Chapter 17. Operations

## Defining How You Operate

Operations in your business is a big area. It can represent literally every process (or the work you do without a process) in your business.

For the sake of brevity, we're going to consider operations as consisting of three major things:

Anything you do to create or prepare your product.

Anything you do to delivery your product.

Anything you do to service and support your product.

In order to achieve scale, you need to define these three processes and call them your Critical Operational Processes.

Even if you deliver a service, you will certainly have some kind of creation or preparation process before you deliver it. You need to be able to define what the process is and create a system for it.

Most business owners find they spend a great deal of time preparing to deliver a product whereas this work can be automated or done by someone else. In order to identify the steps required to deliver the product, create a workflow diagram of what it takes to get ready to deliver. Make sure the diagram accurately reflects the order of steps and whether or not one step needs to precede another.

To get started, we list all the steps required to deliver the product. Don't worry about order at this point. For example, in order to deliver a speech to a local organization, your process may look something like the following:

Finalize date and topic with client

Arrange travel

Get information about the space, logistics, etc.

Write speech

Rehearse and time speech

Call forty-eight hours in advance to get confirmation

Travel to event

Next, we take the steps and arrange them in order while also keeping track of which step is required before moving to the next step. This may mean that we have different tracks of tasks. Parallel tracks are not uncommon. Many business owners have parallel tracks but don't know it. Since they try to execute the tasks in order without thinking about the parallel tasks, they feel like they have to do it all. We'll see why that's not true.

Our speech example may look like this:

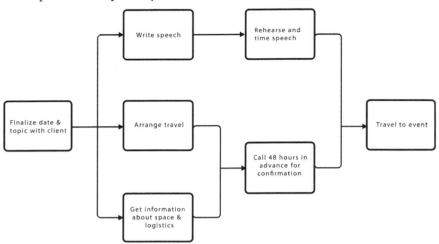

*Figure 8. Operations Process Diagram for Giving a Speech*

You'll notice there are three parallel paths. That means these tasks can be done independently of each other. That's important, because when we begin to manage this new process, we need to know which tasks are dependent upon other tasks.

The next thing you need to think about is the skill set required to handle each task. To make things simple, you are going to classify each task into three buckets:

A task that I – and only I can perform.

A task that someone else could handle eventually, but for the next few years only I can do this.

A task that – with the appropriate training – someone else can handle.

We're going to use color coding to help us see where we can free ourselves up.

The first type of task is red. The second is yellow. The third is green.

Now, you can color code the diagram.

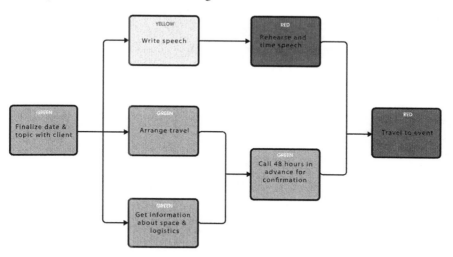

*Figure 9. Color-Coded Operations Process Diagram for Delivering a Speech*

This visual gives us great insight into what we need to spend our time doing and what we don't need to be doing.

Your job now is to find someone to do all the green tasks and start thinking about how to transition out of the yellow boxes.

What if your diagram is all red?

First of all, when my clients draw their diagrams, I challenge every red box. I ask the question, "What would happen if you were unavailable or otherwise unable to do this task?" Unless the answer is, "We would be unable to deliver the product or service", then something that appears red is really yellow (or even green).

Most business owners have difficulty letting go of tasks they think are uniquely their responsibility. But a business that scales is about process, not skill set. You need to think of yourself as the inventor of a process and intellectual property, not a service or product. Unless you can successfully hand off that service to someone else, you will be always be trapped in your business.

What about this speech diagram? It has red boxes.

True, it does (for now). Later in this chapter we're going to talk about how to improve the process so the entire process is green. At the moment, however, we're simply defining how to operate in the short- and medium-term. That means finding green boxes where they didn't exist before, and admitting that some of the boxes that you think are red are really yellow.

Repeat this exercise for the other two areas: product delivery, and product service and support. It may take you some time to think through each process.

Don't be tempted to go straight for the diagram. In my experience, most business owners who don't brainstorm first miss steps, or put several steps together in one box. It's easier to do a brainstorming exercise on the steps before drawing a diagram.

# Coordinating with a Team

Let's focus on the green boxes.

These are the tasks that a team can handle. You will need to assemble that team, which means automating, outsourcing, or hiring (we'll focus on outsourcing and hiring in the next chapter). For now, we're going to talk about how to integrate processes and people.

Integrating a team requires three steps.

1.  Training
2.  Systems
3.  Accountability

## *Training*

Training is the first critical element to success. I'll spend more time on it in the next chapter, but for tasks you currently perform and are ready to hand off, there is one foolproof way to train a new person: make a video of yourself performing the task.

If the task is online, do a screen-capture recording. Otherwise, just record yourself performing the task. That way, after you introduce the task to the person, they can watch you do it and review it at their leisure.

Create a shared area where you record and upload training videos. That way, once you make a decision to outsource a task, the next time you perform it will be the last. Even if you haven't chosen who will perform the task, record yourself performing it and talking through the process. It will force you to think about the skill set required, and will help during the interview process.

## *Systems*

The most common complaint I hear from business owners trying to integrate new people into their business is: "They just didn't do what I asked them to do!" Sometimes it's because the person didn't receive good instructions.

I always ask, "What was your system?" I often get blank stares. They usually say something like, "Well, I gave a deadline, and the deadline just passed. Do I have to follow-up on everything?"

The problem is that with the right system in place, no follow-up would be needed. Things happen when the system kicks in.

So what kind of magical system ensures that things get done? Project management systems. And when they don't get done, you can find out why.

I love project management systems when working with teams. My favorite is Asana, but there are others like Trello and Basecamp. You should find a system that works for you and apply it to your process.

With Asana, you can take a process, break it into steps, assign those steps to people, assign deadlines, attach documents and notes to help, and get instant feedback about this step is in the process. Many other systems offer similar functionality.

The difference comes in when you ensure that the deadline is built not just into the system but also into the process.

For example, if you have a designer who needs to provide a new image for social sharing to your social media staff; the social media staff should be expecting it. Normally, they get informed once it arrives. But since this is a process for delivering your product or handling your marketing, they are aware of where they stand in the process, what they're waiting for, and when it should arrive. If it doesn't arrive on time, they can reach out to whomever is responsible for the previous step and ask about it. That way, each stage of the process is responsible for moving the things along so you don't find out that one step "blew it" only once you're at the end.

## *Accountability*

Sometimes, things just aren't going to work; that's normal. But there needs to be accountability for your people if they don't do what they're supposed to do.

It's easy, as a business owner, to let things slide and pick up the slack, yourself. I talk to many business owners who tell me that when their people don't get stuff done, they just do it themselves rather than take the time to correct the problem.

In the short-term, fixing it yourself is easier, but you shouldn't have to do that each and every time. If you fix it once, it should stay fixed; if not, it's time for you to find new help. Either way, you're better off holding your people accountable for their tasks and teaching them how to perform them.

When one member of your staff doesn't follow through on their assignment, you need to act, but act reasonably. We will discuss problem resolution in the next chapter, but the important thing to remember is to address the situation directly. Don't let it go. It may be as simple as explaining the importance of the task or it may turn out that the individual didn't understand how to handle the task. Which situation is which takes some care and patience on your part to determine, but spending the time working it through will pay dividends as you are able to get rid of low-value tasks that keep you from building your business.

For a more in-depth explanation about how to integrate a team into your business, see Chris Ducker's book, *Virtual Freedom*. I highly recommend it as a way to learn how to start offloading tasks to others.

## Improving the Process

Once you've defined the process, it's now time to improve upon it. There are three types of improvement we're going to focus on:

1. Efficiency Improvements

2. Re-design to Make Yourself Unnecessary

3. Complete Re-engineering

### *Efficiency Improvements*

Turn back to your process diagram from earlier, the one without the colors on it. The first question you should ask is whether there is a way to reduce the steps in your process.

There are two major ways to reduce steps: you can either eliminate unnecessary steps, or you can condense steps.

Let's address the first issue. You might think there are no unnecessary steps in your process, but take a moment to think about it. Often, processes grow over time. And things get added to the process in response to events that occur every day.

You might be surprised to discover that some of what you do is redundant – simply not necessary. Find a way to remove those steps.

There may also be ways to condense a series of existing steps. Take a look at your diagram and find a long row of steps connected to each other. This series of steps is ripe for efficiency.

Investigate the steps and see if there is another way to accomplish them in a single step.

For example, perhaps you have two steps where in the first step, a researcher finds information and delivers it via spreadsheet to you, while in a second step, another worker takes the spreadsheet and uploads it into a database. You can easily combine these steps into one with the right person or technology. Simply teach the researcher to upload the data from the spreadsheet.

## Re-Design to Make Yourself Unnecessary

It's time to take a look at our red boxes. You may think red boxes are red because they simply cannot be changed, but a scaled business has no red boxes.

Did you hear that? No. Red. Boxes.

You goal should be to make you completely unnecessary from the business.

Let's take the example we've been studying. The red boxes were for rehearsing and traveling. Surely there is no way to turn those boxes green. But actually, by rethinking our Business Model, we can hire speakers to deliver our intellectual property or license it out to others. And now, guess what? Even those red boxes are now green.

Your eventual goal should be to turn all of the boxes green.

There is usually only one reason why a box should remain red: you have specialized knowledge or skills. There are two ways to handle that problem: train, or productize.

If you decide that your specialized knowledge can be transferred to others, you can take the steps to bring others onto your team so that they deliver the content instead of you.

However, sometimes you might decide that your specialized knowledge cannot be transferred easily; perhaps it was created over time or built up from a unique set of experiences. If that's the case, you will need to productize your knowledge in order to deliver it in an automated and scaled way to remove yourself from the process.

Here are some ideas for re-design what you do to make yourself unnecessary.

1.  Hire and train someone to do what you do.

2.  Automate what you do.

3.  Take your expertise and turn it into intellectual property. License it and have others deliver it.

4.  Change your delivery mechanism from live to recorded, or via book or webinar.

5.  Remove (undesired) travel and deliver remotely.

This list is just a starting point to think about how to remove yourself from your business.

## *Complete Re-Engineering*

This is the fun part.

Here, we wipe the slate clean and re-draw the boxes from scratch. In order to re-engineer the process, we start with the end result we want to achieve and erase every other box on the diagram.

Re-engineering is a brainstorming exercise. Since you've been trapped in an old process for so long, it's a good idea to enlist other people in your brainstorming process; get fresh ideas involved.

Here's how to run a re-engineering brainstorming session:

First, focus on your outcome; don't think about the tasks required to achieve your outcome.

Second, create tasks that combine information gathering with information usage. As in the above example of the researcher, don't create two steps when one will do. If you need to gather information and then use it, make that one step.

Third, pretend that people who are separated or virtual are really sitting together. For example, if you have two virtual assistants who pass information between them, think about how the process would be different if they were in the same room. Would they still pass from one to the next or would they work together and do it at the same time?

Fourth, make decisions when information is created. If quality control or approvals are needed, make sure they are in place or acquired as close to the completion of the task as possible. In fact, automating the approval or quality control is even better.

Fifth, capture information once and only once. Think about the information you need to gather for the process. Get it all at once. If you have to go back to the source over and over again you are building in inefficiencies.

## EXERCISE 17.1 MAPPING YOUR OPERATIONS FOR PRODUCT CREATION AND DELIVERY

1. Brainstorm all the steps necessary to create or prepare for delivery of your product. If you have multiple products, just start with your biggest seller.

_____

_____

_____

_____

2. Create a workflow map using the steps above putting them in order and showing which tasks precede others.

Color in your workflow map with three colors: red, for tasks you must do yourself; yellow, for tasks which someone else could eventually do, but for the next few years you will do alone; and green, for tasks which someone else could do - if trained appropriately.

## EXERCISE 17.2 MAPPING YOUR OPERATIONS FOR PRODUCT DELIVERY

1. Brainstorm all the steps necessary to deliver your product. If you have multiple products, just start with your biggest seller.

_____

_____

_____

_____

2. Create a workflow map using the steps above putting them in order and showing which tasks precede others.

Color in your workflow map with three colors: red, for tasks you must do yourself; yellow, for tasks which someone else could eventually do, but for the next few years you will do alone; and green, for tasks which someone else could do - if trained appropriately.

## EXERCISE 17.3 MAPPING YOUR OPERATIONS FOR PRODUCT SERVICE AND SUPPORT

1. Brainstorm all the steps necessary to service and support your product. If you have multiple products, just start with your biggest seller.

_____

_____

_____

_____

2. Create a workflow map using the steps above putting them in order and showing which tasks precede others.

Color in your workflow map with three colors: red, for tasks you must do yourself; yellow, for tasks which someone else could eventually do, but for the next few years you will do alone; and green, for tasks which someone else could do - if trained appropriately.

# Chapter 18. The People

## Hiring

Scaling your business may require you to add staff. Whether you're thinking of hiring your first employee or your fiftieth, I find that most entrepreneurs approach the task with either fear or frustration.

The first question most small business owners ask me is: how do I know when it's the right time to bring someone on?

The best answer I've ever heard was given by Michael Port, the *New York Times* #1 Best-Selling Author of the book, *Book Yourself Solid*. His reply was, "If you're thinking about it, it's probably time."

I find that to be true most of the time. If the idea of hiring help has crossed your mind, then your mind is telling you something. Of course, you should be prudent in your hiring practices, spending only what you can afford for assistance. And you don't have to go "all in" and hire a full-time employee. There are many ways of getting assistance without breaking the bank.

I had the opportunity to sit down with Mel West, owner of Prosperity Logic. Mel is an executive coach and an expert at organizational development. I asked him what the biggest mistake is that people make when they hire their first employee.

"A lot of entrepreneurs hire a friend because it's easier or cheaper," Mel said.

I can attest to this trend, not just from what I've seen but from my own experience. Although it's tempting to expand your dream by extending it to work with people you like, this can be really problematic.

First of all, is your friend really the best qualified for the job? If not, why start there? And if you're making a choice based on what's cheap, you will feel the impact when you have to re-do work or re-explain tasks several times rather than get the right person for the job in the first place.

On the flip side, there's no reason to go out and hire an expensive, full-time resource if you don't need it. Find the resource to match the need.

Before you can hire someone, you need to have a documented process that is going to be handed off. That's why we spent the last chapter focusing on process documentation and improvement. Another big mistake entrepreneurs make is hiring someone before the tasks are well-defined. That's just a recipe for disaster. Make sure you know exactly what needs to be handed-off and have those procedures and steps well-documented for someone to understand.

If you don't know which tasks need to be handed off, Mel has a few suggestions for where to start.

"Start with those tasks you don't like to do. They're probably the ones that aren't getting done. After that, think about those tasks that need more attention. They should be where you start."

Recruiting can be a big job and is intimidating for many business owners, but it doesn't have to be. Instead of trying to write down a full job description, Mel suggests writing down three to five key accountabilities. These are the tasks which the person will be responsible for and executing well six months from now. Painting a vision of what the person will be doing after training is over is a very good way of communicating to candidates what the job is and your expectations.

Interviewing candidates over the phone or Skype is a critical step to successful employee selection. There are a number of interview techniques, but one of the most effective is asking scenario-based, open-ended questions to confirm the skill sets and attitudes of the employee.

Identify three or four scenarios that will make up the majority of the future employee's work. Ask open-ended questions about how the candidate would handle those scenarios. Be sure to focus on scenarios involving the exact tasks and situations you're trying to avoid.

For example, if you are trying to hire someone because there's never any time to do lead generation, make sure to ask about how they would perform that task. But above and beyond that, make sure to ask how they would continue with lead generation if you don't have time to assist them. Would the work continue or would it grind to a halt? This question is critical because you're hiring someone to stop you from being the bottleneck. If you're still the bottleneck after the person is in place, what was the point?

While assessing the experience and skill of the candidate over the phone, avoid Yes and No questions; they rarely tell you anything, and simply tell the candidate to confirm your bias in the question. When weighing the difference between attitude versus skill, you can always teach skills but you can rarely change attitudes. Hire for attitude above all else.

## Training

Once you've made a decision to bring an employee or contractor on board, it's now up to you to train them to be successful at their job. During the training sequence, keep in mind that you already have quantified what success looks like for this job. The success criteria are contained in the three to five key accountabilities you defined for this role.

Mel has a unique view on implementing employee training. He describes a training program as a "mentoring program." Most entrepreneurs do not think of training a new employee as mentoring, but if you consider what you're doing, you're trying to replace yourself, or at least part of yourself. This new employee is going to be executing your vision and growing into a role so that your business can run without you.

Mentoring is about helping people grow into a new role. If you view what you're doing as mentoring rather than training, you will see the time spent as an investment, not only in your future but in your employee's, as well. This kind of thinking aligns your goals with your employee's.

Keep in mind that your employee is going to have to learn from you. Mel tells us this works best when your employee learns the same way you do. Keep this in mind during the recruiting process. If you learn best through visual training, then you're more likely to create video tutorials. Having an employee that learns best this way, too, is a bonus.

Because you spent the time to document your procedures before you hired a new employee (you did that, right?), you can now share that documentation with your new employee. Some really effective ways of training your employee include:

- Creating video tutorials of key tasks with a screen share and voiceover explanation.

- Videotaping yourself performing the task

- Documenting processes and procedures in a project management tool like Asana.

- Having your employee shadow you on a task to observe one complete cycle.

- Holding regular meetings with the employee to answer questions and clarify tasks.

Keep in mind that you will be spending a great deal of time at the beginning of your employee's relationship with your company teaching them how to do what you need them to do. In fact, it will likely require more time than it would simply take to do the job yourself.

Don't make the mistake of giving up or pulling away from the task until your employee is ready. Even if they are an expert in their field, don't assume they know how to do the task the way *you* want them to perform it or in the way that will be most successful for your business.

If you're looking for a set of steps to kick off a successful training program, here are some that can work:

1. Share with your new employee the three to five key accountabilities you have created (in writing).

2. Share with your new employee all of the procedures you've documented (in writing).

3. If you haven't done so already, create video tutorials on each task required for the process you are delegating. Share it with the new employee.

4. Set up a regular meeting with the employee to share your vision, answer questions, and make sure things are going well.

5. Allow for a reasonable amount of mistakes during the first period. Be generous with praise; be stingy with criticism.

6. After a reasonable period of time, have an accountability meeting to assess how things are going.

7. Set goals for the next period.

8. Repeat.

## Leadership

This section was originally titled "Management," but I was convinced that this is the wrong way to think about the concept.

Mel put it perfectly: "You manage processes. You lead people."

If the concept of leadership feels foreign to you, it may make sense to invest in leadership training. If you are planning on bringing people into your organization, you will need to have leadership skills.

The most popular place to learn about leadership is through the Dale Carnegie Course. But there are a few other options. The Leadership Challenge is a program that approaches creating leaders with measurable, learnable, teachable behaviors. (You can learn more at leadershipchallenge.com.) Another program is the Leadership Circle. The Leadership Circle approach goes beyond the normal assessments and descriptions to provide actionable steps to acquire effective leadership skills. One coach I personally know who provides this training is Jason Billows. You can read more about him at jasonbillowsleadership.com.

Because it's easier to recognize a bad leader than a good one, here are three big mistakes leaders make with new employees.

1. Not being ready to delegate or train a new employee.
2. Micromanaging employees.
3. Over-focusing on the "bad" and not emphasizing the "good."

The first issue is, of course, avoidable. As I have discussed earlier, do not hire a new employee until you are ready. Ready means knowing exactly which tasks need to be delegated, and documenting each task. Enough said.

Micromanaging is usually a lack of trust or a lack of self-confidence. The problem with micromanagers is that they do not know they are micromanagers so you need to dig deep here.

Here are five signs you're a micromanager as presented by Harvard Business Review and Muriel Maignan Wilkins:[3]

---

[3] https://hbr.org/ 2014/11/signs-that-youre-a-micromanager

1. You're never quite satisfied with the work that's being done.

2. You feel frustrated because you would have done the work differently — not necessarily achieve a different outcome but pursue a different process.

3. You focus in on the details, and immediately start correcting them.

4. You always want to know what people are working on.

5. You ask for updates quite frequently.

6. You like to be copied on e-mails and other communication so you can just be "looped in."

If this sounds like you, you need to change what you do. Micromanaging is not "just another management style." It's bad. It's bad for you and your staff.

Think about yourself here. Do you not trust your people? Or do you just feel insecure about delegating these tasks to other people? These are not easy questions, but you will not be successful growing your business if you can't trust others or if you're insecure. Period. Get yourself a business coach or a life coach to work through these issues. Get them behind you and improve your leadership skills.

Finally, even good leaders can over focus on the "bad." Often people think that the job of a good leader is to provide "constructive criticism" and that praise doesn't help people grow.

Nothing could be further from the truth.

Without praise, your employee has no basis upon which to grow.

Feedback is important. You need to help guide your new employee to improve their performance.

But everyone is going to make mistakes. You need to realize that eight good outcomes and one bad outcome is a good outcome. For everything you want to criticize, count the outcomes and make sure your reaction is proportional to the entire experience.

Good leadership requires you to create an atmosphere of shared accountability. You need to be accountable, and your employees should feel like they can hold you accountable. When accountability runs both ways, your business will be operating on shared metrics – Key Performance Indicators – you have set as a team. These KPIs should be SMART goals – Specific, Measurable, Assignable, Realistic, and Time-related.

Accountability requires follow-up. One big mistake new leaders make is to set expectations but never follow up on them. You need to create an atmosphere in which follow-up is expected and valued.

Honing your leadership skills takes work. But it pays off many times over with a loyal and productive team at your side as you grow your business with partners that pick up the slack.

## Problem Resolution

Mark my words. It will happen.

You will eventually have to resolve problems with people.

Many entrepreneurs find this their biggest challenge because they are so used to working alone.

Mel gives us a few tips about problem resolution. His advice: think about how you would want to be treated.

If you are working with a client or another group and something isn't going right, wouldn't you want someone to let you know? Clearly, you would want them to let you know kindly.

The key problem is that most of us are programmed to assume that if something isn't happening, it's because the person didn't want to do the job. And that hits us deeply and personally. It feels like a betrayal of sorts. After all, we invited someone into our vision, dedicated our time and effort to train them, and this is how they repay us?

Obviously, we need to hold off on going to that dark place for a few minutes, and think about the facts.

There are many reasons why there are problems in business. I like to think of it as a grid in two dimensions: "Skill" and "Will". Either something can't be done, or someone doesn't want to do it.

But there's another dimension. "Skill" and "Will" issues can occur within an individual, a group of employees, or be organizational in nature. The combination of these two dimensions gives us six total root causes of problems. Let's look at each.

| | Skill | Will |
|---|---|---|
| **Organization** | Lack of Tools | Financial & Other Incentives |
| **Group** | Bad Environment | Others Undermine |
| **Individual** | Training | Motivation |

*Figure 10. Finding the Root Cause of a Personnel Problem*

At the personal level, the level most business owners are familiar with, the problems are familiar.

213

<u>Personal Skill problems</u> refer to the person involved not knowing how to accomplish a given task. Perhaps the training isn't sufficient for the individual, or the person doesn't have the tools to accomplish the task.

<u>Personal Will problems</u> are the ones most business owners think are happening, but that's usually not the problem. This problem occurs when the individual simply doesn't want to do the task or isn't motivated.

<u>Group Skill problems</u> occur when the employees that the individual is around do not provide the proper environment for completing the task. For example, perhaps your employee is supposed to post content on your blog, but your writers do not provide the content in a timely or usable manner. Here, the group is trying to complete the task, but the system between employees is broken.

<u>Group Will problems</u> occur when the employees around the individual undermine the task. For example, your instructions may be that all blog posts include three references, but in casual conversation, the other employees say that this isn't necessary or that no one really does it. So the employee also doesn't do it. The group – as a whole – doesn't have the will to complete the task.

<u>Organizational Skill problems</u> occur when you, as the business owner, don't provide the tools to complete the task. For example, you ask your employee to post articles on your social media account but you do not provide the employee with tools to curate those articles.

<u>Organizational Will problems</u> occur when you do not incent the right behavior. For example, you want your salespeople to bring profitable deals, but you incent them on the volume of business they bring, not the profitability of that business. So, you cannot be surprised when you receive a lot of low-priced business.

Knowing that issues can result from these six potential problems, you should approach problem resolution with your employees as a "fact-finding mission." Your first conversation should be to gather information so you can decide which of these six items is interfering with task completion. Only then can you address the underlying cause.

## Dismissal

Even after all of this, you may eventually come to the determination that it's time to separate an employee from your company. Or, you may be forced to do it because of financial conditions. Letting an employee go is probably the worst management task you can have and it's the fear of every entrepreneur who hires employees.

But if it happens and is done well, you can make it a less agonizing experience all around.

Mel gives us some tips.

Let people go on a Monday morning. This is contrary to the conventional wisdom of letting people go on Friday afternoons. Mel says Monday mornings allow people to have the entire week to find the resources they need to take care of themselves.

Fire somebody on a Friday and they spend two whole days stewing about it, worrying about how they're going to pay their bills, and without access to any resources. Monday through Friday, people can apply for unemployment benefits, check job prospects, and talk to other companies, and it makes them feel like they're closing the gap: making progress.

Finally, allow someone to exit with dignity. Tell the truth; the whole truth. If layoffs are occurring because of bad business decisions, take responsibility for them. Just because you're responsible doesn't mean it doesn't happen. You still need to do what's right for your business, but at least be accountable for your part.

If someone has to go because they're not working out, be honest about why they're not working out. If you feel that you can offer a reference letter, offer it; if not, then don't. But don't debate or argue with the employee. They're leaving your organization. Trying to educate them about what they did or didn't do isn't worth it at this point.

In the end, it comes down to Mel's advice at the beginning: treat people how you would like to be treated, and all will end well.

## EXERCISE 18.1 HIRING YOUR STAFF

1. List tasks that are required for your business that you do not like to perform. _____

_____

_____

_____

2. List tasks that are required for your business that aren't getting enough attention. _____

_____

_____

_____

3. Between the two lists above, identify a role that can handle these tasks - or at least the majority of these tasks. The role might be administrative or marketing or sales or technical. But choose a role (or roles) that will cover the tasks you wish to outsource. _____

_____

4. Write 3 to 5 key accountabilities for the new staff member. These will describe what the employee will be expected and able to do 6 months into the job.

_____

_____

_____

_____

5. Think of the tasks required to perform the key accountabilities listed above. What is the state of the documentation of these tasks? Are they documented or are they in your head? Plan what you will do to create solid documentation for these tasks.

_____

_____

_____

6. Think of 4 scenarios you will ask about in the interview that are likely to come up during the course of the employee's work.

_____

_____

_____

_____

_____

_____

# Section 6. The New Road

# Chapter 19. Feedback and Change

## Continuous Improvement

The only constant is change. And, of course, in your business you need to not only be ready for it, but lead it.

Everything I've talked about in terms of creating your scalable business is a system. And systems need improvement.

There are two ways you can go about improving your systems. You can wait until things start breaking and you're forced to improve your system, or you can be prepared to make small improvements as you go.

I prefer the latter.

There is a lot written on continuous process improvement and some of the information varies between sources, but most of it is centered on a four-step process for improvement.

1.  Plan: identify an opportunity and plan to take advantage of it.

2.  Do: execute your plan.

3.  Check: see if the plan you execute produced the outcome you wanted.

4.  Act: if it worked, find another opportunity. If not, go back and change your plan.

Of all the steps above, checking is usually the one that's hardest to execute. To implement a continuous process improvement model in your business, you need to have a system in place to check whether what you're doing actually produced the outcome you expected.

But let's review them all.

## Plan

You should always be looking for opportunities to improve. Things don't get better by themselves. You have to have something specific that you're working on.

One of the most difficult things for business owners to do is identify the one thing they should be fixing right now. As entrepreneurs, we tend to be a bit distracted.

But you can really only do one thing at a time. Not just because you need to focus on something with laser-like precision, but because changing more than one thing at a time won't let you determine if what you changed was really the problem.

Think about it this way: if your sales are starting to slump and you decide to change your messaging *and* your product at the same time, when things start getting better, what was the reason? Was it the messaging? Or was it the new product? Or was it both?

You can't know when you change too many variables at once.

Once you've identified what you're going to change, you need to develop a hypothesis about what should happen. If this sounds like a science class from school, you're right. You should run your growing business like a science experiment. Test something and see what happens. But have an idea about your goal or desired outcome in advance. That way you can develop a plan to achieve that goal.

## Do

This step should be self-explanatory, but unfortunately, it often gets lost. Your plan needs to be executed over a particular period of time.

Choose the date the change should go into effect and build up to it. Then execute it – on time.

Don't be afraid of the change. If things don't go well, you can always change back. Rarely are things irreversible in business. But you'll never know if you should change until you try.

## Check

Part of your planning exercise should be figuring out how you'll measure the metric you've chosen to see if your plan was successful. Every change you make in your company should be aligned a very specific metric.

Make the change. Measure the metric.

Give it some time before you draw a conclusion. How much time depends on which metric you're measuring and how much data you're collecting.

For example, if you get 1000 visitors a day to your landing page, it won't take more than a day or two to see if a change you made positively affected your conversion rate. But if you only get thirty visitors a day, you may need to wait longer.

There's no magic rule about when you have enough information to evaluate. Some A/B Testing tools (comparing two slightly different versions) give you the statistical validity of your test results. For example, LeadPages will tell you the statistical probability that version B performs better than your current version A.

But mostly you just need to use some judgment. Don't react too quickly, but don't wait too long either. In principle, you can react more quickly to a positive change than to no change at all.

For example, if you do A/B Testing of a landing page and see that your new version performs better after a few days and more than fifty or so visitors to the page, you can be almost certain your new version will outperform the old one. However, if version B is getting about the same conversion rate as the original, you may have to wait longer to determine if version B is adding anything.

The important thing is to measure, and check your hypothesis.

## Act

If you learn that a change is necessary, then make it. In the landing page example, once you learn that version B outperforms your original page, get rid of the old in favor of the new – quickly.

Don't waste time once you've determined it's time to move on.

## Feedback from the Market

One of the most important things you can do as a business owner is listen to the marketplace. I've already talked about listening to your customers to make sure they're satisfied and getting their feedback on your products.

We listen to the marketplace in order to improve. Let's look at a few ways we can implement continuous process improvement by listening to the marketplace. It impacts many of the processes I've showed you so far.

## Improving Messaging through A/B Testing

Believe it or not, your messaging is a process. You have defined audience segments, and you created messages for them that you think will be meaningful. Now you have to check to see if, in fact, they were meaningful.

This means you'll be measuring the impact of your messages to see if prospects are responding to your calls-to-action. This means measuring response rates.

But more than that, we need to see if one message is better than another. So not only do we need to measure response rates, but we need a mechanism for comparing one message to the other. That requires what is often referred to as A/B Testing or Split Testing.

Maybe you have one message that has a slightly different headline from the other, or one appears in a different color. You launch both options and see which one performs better.

Many marketing tools have A/B Testing capabilities built in. LeadPages allows you to implement A/B Testing on your landing pages so you can hone in on one that performs best.

But as is often the case with continuous improvement methods, the testing really never ends. You're always going to be testing one thing or another to see if you can get better results. Messaging is no exception. Just because you find one message that works doesn't mean it couldn't be improved. In fact, months later, it may need to be changed completely.

And you won't know unless you have the process in place to test.

## Improving Product through User Feedback

Once you've developed the minimal viable product (MVP) and gone to market, you'll start to add functionality. But you'll want a process in place to assess which functions you should add and which will not improve your sales.

User groups are perfect for this kind of feedback. You can certainly do market research and survey prospects about what they want, but your best information comes from paying customers.

Paying customers are motivated to help you be successful. Have you ever had a restaurant you loved and watched it go out of business? It's frustrating, isn't it? Your users will feel the same way if you can't keep their product in the market.

Don't just survey customers randomly. Invite customers to join a user group that they commit to and where they are expected to give feedback on a regular basis. User groups have a format, and they have meetings. Even if they're virtual, at first, hold meetings with your user groups to get feedback. Ask them what they're missing. Talk to them about how they're using your product. Ask them what else they're currently buying, especially if it's being used with your product.

These are all new feature ideas.

It's important to test your new product ideas with your user group. Give away the new features to a test audience and see how they interact with them. Don't over-rely on survey results because they can be notoriously misleading.

*Money talks. Everything else is just data.*

## Improving Your Marketing System through Metric Management

I've spent some time discussing the importance of metrics and understanding how well your marketing system performs. It's not enough to measure it if you don't manage it. Management means seeing the places where you can improve and making the changes.

For example, if you usually have steady growth in your e-mail list but suddenly it starts to plateau, that tells you that something needs to be improved. If you don't monitor that information on a regular basis, you will only find out after your revenue is affected. By then, it's usually quite late in the game.

Continuous process improvement in marketing systems can be handled through a marketing dashboard. No company is too small to have a marketing dashboard, even if it's something as simple as Google Analytics or your Infusionsoft Dashboard. You should have key metrics from your campaigns and measure them on a regular basis. Any change should be acted upon immediately.

The main point behind continuous process improvement is to check and act. Clearly, you need to plan, but business owners most often forget to see if what they're doing is actually working.

Just because things are going well today doesn't mean that you stop improving. There's always opportunity to improve. And even if the metrics are good, customer feedback will show you where you can improve.

Continuous process improvement isn't a destination; it's a journey. It's an organizational skill you put into place at your business. Once in place, you live the principles every day. The best organizations do it; yours should as well.

## Organizational Change Model

There are a number of different organizational change models and I'm not going to pick between them. Teaching you how to guide your new and growing organization through change is beyond the scope of this book.

Instead, I want to focus on a more basic model of change. As you lead your organization, you need to wrap the concept of continuous process improvement in a preparation and reinforcement phase. It should look like this:

- Prepare the organization
- Execute continuous process improvement
  (Plan. Do. Check. Act.)
- Reinforce the change with the organization

Instead of going through dozens of different kinds of change models, simply wrap your process improvement in a "change sandwich."

## Prepare the Organization

No one likes surprises. And the longer you've been doing something, the more likely you're going to resist doing it differently. So, preparing the organization for change isn't a new employee problem; it's more often a long-term employee problem, people who've gotten used to "always doing it the same way."

If you have employees, make sure you explain exactly what you're doing. If you're changing something that you're going to test, make sure people understand that it's a test. Make sure that people understand exactly what's going to change and if it's temporary, how long it will last.

Even small things that people don't have a lot to do with on a day-to-day basis can represent big changes to what they do. If expectations aren't met, or a regular routine isn't satisfied, people get nervous. Any time you have an opportunity to make people feel more comfortable with a change, not only are they going to be more comfortable in their jobs, but they're going to feel a sense of ownership over their job and the process, as well.

Preparing the organization for change also means understanding exactly what the implications of the change are going to be. Make sure you take the time to talk with the appropriate staff members to understand the downstream impacts of all of the changes you're planning to make. You might be surprised to find out how one small thing, which seemingly isn't related to anything else, can have a huge impact.

For example, you might want to do A/B (or "Split") Testing on the messaging of a landing page, only to find out that that same message is core to downstream sales messages that are included in autoresponder e-mails. Making a change in one place might actually need to show results in a number of different places – throughout your website or throughout e-mails – so make sure you talk to everyone who might be involved so you know that you've taken all of the variables into consideration.

Preparing the organization also involves getting people's feedback – employee's feedback. By asking your staff members what they think about a certain change, or asking for ideas that might make the change easier to implement or more effective, will go a long way towards achieving the outcome that you're expecting, as well as keeping everyone in the loop and having them feel a sense of ownership.

Open and honest communication with the organization is the best way to make sure that people are not resistant to the change that you're making, and they actually feel like partners and owners in the change itself.

## Reinforce the Change in the Organization

Once you've gone through the cycle of change and have implemented a new procedure in your company, you need to reinforce it. Announce your decision to everyone involved – everyone at the company and especially those who are involved in the change. Make sure they know that the change is now permanent, especially if it came out of a testing routine.

It's very frustrating for employees who are involved in a test to find out that the test is finished and now things are either permanent or have rolled back without their understanding what happened and why. Make sure everyone understands that you've implemented a new way of doing things, and that you're not going back to the old way.

You can reinforce the change in a couple of different ways. First of all, it's important that any processes related to the old way of doing things are gone. If you decide to implement a new project management system, and people used to send tasks back and forth via e-mail, it's important that tasks no longer be sent via e-mail. In fact, it's important that every employee enforce this rule by replying back to anyone who tries to use the old process and informing them that they would prefer to use the new process. If specific company resources were used – for example, maybe your company used a specific type of spreadsheet – make sure to get rid of that spreadsheet so that people can't go back to using the old process accidentally.

The desire to revert to the old way of doing things is very powerful and shouldn't be underestimated. You need to make sure that you don't allow this to happen and don't give any kind of an allowance. Once you've made a decision that a change has to be made, it must to stay in place until you change your mind. It's perfectly fine to change your mind and go back to an old way if you decide that the new way is not working well, but make sure that this decision is announced to the entire company, so that they can expect that as future changes occur you will announce them, as opposed to giving your employees the sense that you may change your mind randomly.

This is a very important point, because if you leave the impression that you don't really stick to your decisions, the next time you need to make a significant change, those who oppose it will simply wait you out and all of the efforts that you've spent in preparing your organization and executing the change will be for naught.

Finally, reinforcing the change may also require talking to individuals who are not toeing the line. If you have individuals within your organization who refuse to accommodate the change or are having trouble doing so, you may need to pull them aside in a one-on-one conversation to talk about the problem. Don't let individuals ruin the organizational change you're trying to put in place. It can be detrimental to the morale of the organization as well as the outcome you're trying to achieve.

If your change is part of a test and there's part of the organization that won't go along with the test, your results will not be accurate and you won't be able to learn if there's something you can improve in your organization. It's important that you lead the change.

Once your company becomes bigger, the change may actually be proposed by another part of your organization. If that's the case, and you agree with that direction, it's important that you lead by example. Everyone will look to the head of the company to determine whether or not the change is real and is going to stick, or if it's simply a passing fancy of a middle level manager.

The bottom line is clear: scaling your company requires change, and not just one change, but a sequence of changes that will occur over time. In order to scale your company, you're going to have to get good at change. You'll need to learn to embrace it. Business owners that have difficulty with change or don't like change will have to break this habit or accept change as a learned skill. Every business needs to go through it to survive, and embrace it if they plan to scale.

# Chapter 20. Achieving Scale

## The Next Growth Ceiling

Remember the law of human nature that got us here? Most people aren't happy without progress.

Well, that law of human nature has its good side and its bad. The good side is that it pushes us to be more than we are today. The bad side is that we're going to hit that Growth Ceiling over and over again in our business.

No matter where you are today in your business, after you break through the Growth Ceiling, there will be another one later. Even when you build the right Concept, Business Model, Market, and Processes to scale, you'll be scratching your head again in short order.

But that's great. That means you're continuing to grow; you're undergoing your own business metamorphosis. The trick is seeing it and reacting in time.

So how do you know you're approaching another Growth Ceiling? There are three basic signs:

1. You become more and more frustrated with your work-life balance.

When you hit a Growth Ceiling it's because you are no longer willing to do what you've been doing. Either you've grown, or the company has. Regardless, change is necessary.

It could mean that you're looking for more freedom in your life. It could mean that managing your business the way it is today is no longer of interest. It could also mean that growth has taken your business to a place you hadn't expected.

2. Your marginal costs are increasing.

Remember natural law number one: entropy? Eventually, the changes you put in place will no longer be useful for your business. You'll need to make more changes in order to get entropy under control and start lowering marginal costs.

3. Revenue growth has leveled off for no good reason.

Revenue rises and falls for a lot of reasons. Sometimes it's market conditions; sometimes it's sales performance. But if you've exhausted all the typical reasons and still can't figure out why your numbers are flat-lining, it could be that you've hit another Growth Ceiling. In this case, the market no longer supports your concept and/or Business Model. It's time to go back to the drawing board.

That's a good thing. It means you're ready to move onto the next big thing.

The point is: the Four Keys don't change; you still need a good Concept, Business Model, Market, and Processes to scale. This time around, maybe you need more Process than Concept. Maybe your market needs to expand, or maybe your Business Model needs an additional revenue source. Any way you look at it, they're simply the same categories of work.

Just pull out the book and start the exercises again.

## Getting More Help

There are definitely those who have walked this path before. Sometimes, it's critical to find and connect with them. One of the best ways to do that is through a mastermind program or networking group.

I have offered such groups in the past to help connect business owners with peers for accountability, networking, and idea generation. Sometimes those group are open for new entrants, though not always. If you are interested, you can check the current openings at scaletosuccess.com/mastermind.

## Your Next 90 Days

We've gone through the Four Keys of Scale:

1. The Concept
2. The Business Model
3. The Market
4. The Processes

And with these Four Keys, you're ready to grow your company to the next level. Now that you're motivated and excited to move forward, let's plan out what you're going to do over the next ninety days.

## Step 1. Identify your blind spot.

Let's figure out what you need to work on first. Think about the Four Keys of Scale, and let's come up with which one in which have the biggest opportunity for growth.

On a scale of 1 - 5, where 5 is Strongly Agree and 1 is Strongly Disagree, ask yourself the following questions:

### *Concept:*

With the market I serve, the benefit I create for my clients can be delivered either via automation or via others whom I have trained. (1 = Strongly Disagree, 5 = Strongly Agree)

*Business Model:*

I know how to create diverse, stable, and recurring revenue from my concept and client base. (1 = Strongly Disagree, 5 = Strongly Agree)

*Market:*

I know how to generate leads, grow prospects, and close sales without my personal efforts. (1 = Strongly Disagree, 5 = Strongly Agree)

*Processes:*

I have a set of steps which are known and repeatable to prepare to deliver my product or service, deliver my product or service, and support my product or service. (1 = Strongly Disagree, 5 = Strongly Agree)

Take the Key with the lowest score. If you have a tie, start with the first Key, the Concept, and work your way to the Processes in order.

This is your current biggest opportunity.

## Step 2. Fill the Hole

Pick a way to fill the opportunity gap you just prioritized. Here are some ideas:

*Concept*

1. Offer today's target market a different benefit.
2. Offer a different target market your One Big Benefit in a way that is automated or trained.

3. Pivot by using the methods as part of your service to offer a different benefit to your target market.

## Business Model

4. Adjust your pricing from hourly rates to retainers.

5. Create a subscription pricing model.

6. Diversify your income by creating another product.

## Market

7. Go through your marketing materials and hone your four calls-to-action.

8. Go through your website and re-design to maximize migration.

9. Analyze your content marketing strategy for response and migration.

10. Write a book.

11. Launch a podcast.

12. Launch a webinar platform.

## Processes

13. Document your product production process.

14. Launch a lead generation and marketing system.

15. Hire staff to handle some of your administrative tasks.

16. Train and/or hire sales staff to work with your marketing system.

## Step 3. Build the Plan

Based on the strategy you select in Step 2, now you have to get it done.

Create a plan of action by taking the end goal and breaking it down into smaller steps.

If you're confused as to the steps you need to take, find a business coach who has previously done what you're planning. Ask them how to accomplish the task. Better yet, ask them to mentor you so you can grow your business.

Occasionally, I will personally mentor business owners. If that opportunity is currently available, you'll find it at scaletosuccess.com/mentor.

## Step 4. Make It Happen!

Now it's just a matter of doing it.

Get a mastermind group or an accountability group. If you're looking for ideas on where to find one, check out the Scale to Success Mastermind group at: scaletosuccess.com/mastermind.

Your accountability partners can help you stay on track to accomplish your 90-day plan.


I'm excited that you've decided to take this journey to scale your business. You'll find that as you build on the Four Keys to Scale and grow a business that requires less of your actual involvement, you will be able to create the business you've always wanted. Rather than being tied to your phone or e-mail, you will have an asset that pays off for the rest of your life.

Imagine what that would mean for you. Would that mean vacations with your friends and family? Would that mean time to pursue your hobbies? Would that mean less stress and more freedom?

For me, it was life-changing. No more need to fly all over the world to meet with clients. If I want to travel, I travel because I choose to. I'm able to be home with my family and friends. I can get back into my community and support events and causes I feel passionate about.

And you can to. If you scale.

# About the Author

FRANK H BRIA is a leading authority in helping entrepreneurs scale and grow into the business they always wanted. Frank helps consultants, coaches, and other experts turn their 6-figure practice into a 7-figure business.

He has built and sold tech startups as well as consulted for the largest international corporations in high tech, finance, and retail on 4 continents. Describing himself as a "recovering consultant," Frank now takes what he used to teach the Fortune 500 and applies it to entrepreneurs looking to grow their businesses.

He is an author of several books including Seven Billion Banks and Personalizing Your Marketing. He is host of the podcast Scale to Success. He is also the star of the new TV show Startup Relaunch.

Frank has spoken to audiences across the globe about growing their business. His strategy work is still used by dozens of the largest corporations in the world.

Frank resides with his wife and three daughters in Phoenix, Arizona. When he is not traveling to meet with banks and banking vendors to help them plan for the future of the industry, he enjoys the desert outdoors of Arizona often hiking, camping, and hunting. He also has an interest in foreign languages.

Learn more about Frank at FrankBria.com

Made in the USA
Charleston, SC
05 July 2015